The Clod-Hoppin' Judge

Memoirs of
Judge Gerald Parker Brown

Judge Gerald Parker Brown

iUniverse, Inc.
Bloomington

The Clod-Hoppin' Judge
Memoirs of Judge Gerald Parker Brown

iUniverse books may be ordered through booksellers or by contacting:

iUniverse
1663 Liberty Drive
Bloomington, IN 47403
www.iuniverse.com
1-800-Authors (1-800-288-4677)

Because of the dynamic nature of the Internet, any web addresses or links contained in this book may have changed since publication and may no longer be valid.

Any people depicted in stock imagery provided by Thinkstock are models, and such images are being used for illustrative purposes only.

Certain stock imagery © Thinkstock.

ISBN: 978-1-4620-0309-9 (sc)
ISBN: 978-1-4620-0311-2 (dj)
ISBN: 978-1-4620-0310-5 (ebk)

Printed in the United States of America

iUniverse rev. date: 4/27/2011

Acknowledgments

I can't possibly thank Debra Walker enough for her contribution to this effort. In fact, her contribution has been so critical that she deserves to be listed as co-author. She not only typed the entire manuscript several times; she also made valuable suggestions, and kept the process moving. Suffice it to say that this book would never have seen the light of day but for her. True, that might not have been catastrophic!

Dedication

I dedicate this book to my faithful, ever-loving wife, Lottie Balk Brown, who has enthusiastically supported all my endeavors for more than sixty-six years.

Chapter 1:
Stream of Consciousness Prattle

On the outside chance that my vaporous ruminations might be of passing interest to someone, perhaps my great-great-grandchildren, I'm chronicling some of my experiences during the last 80 percent of the 20th century; some good, some bad; just letting it all hang out, warts and all. If I knew who all, if anyone, may ever read this, I might not admit some of the grosser and more embarrassing episodes, but they are part and parcel of my persona and probably explain why I am who I am. I will further incriminate myself by admitting that I have omitted some of the most scandalous episodes in order to maintain a modicum of good taste. Some may feel that I am telling them more than they want to know but when you get as old as I am, you realize how little you know about your ancestors. Human nature being what it is, when you are young and many ancestors are still alive and possess knowledge about their ancestors, you simply are not interested enough to reap the rich harvest of information available. Not a day goes by now that I don't regret my failure to ask questions that I am intensely interested in now but there is no one alive to help me. I feel that I could enlighten young people on many subjects but they are not interested now. C'est la vie!

I started this dictation in February, 2002, on Abraham Lincoln's birthday, but I originally started writing this paper on January 1, 1995, and entitled it, "Some Notes on the First 75 years of the Life of G.P. Brown." I have added material from time to time through the years and, as a result of that, I am sure there will be some duplication, and some of the episodes will be related out of sequence of their actual happenings. I wrote it on a yellow pad, longhand and shorthand, with many abbreviations which, seven years later, are hard for me to decipher.

Chapter 2:
Family History

I am Gerald Parker Brown and was born in Chalk Bluff Township, Clay County, Arkansas, on August 19, 1920. My parents were Jesse Thomas and Hazel Parker Brown.

My paternal grandfather was Robert Brown, who moved his family from Tennessee to Clay County, and his father was Green Brown, who moved his family from North Carolina to Tennessee. Robert's wife was Martha (Mattie) Hungerford Brown. I believe the Hungerfords came from England. Bob and Mattie had seven children: Jesse, Carl, Edna, Stella, Connie, Ruth and Denver. Jesse and Hazel had five children: Madeline, Mildred, Gerald (me), Reba and Donald.

Hazel's parents were Frank and Rosa Way Parker who moved from Indiana to Arkansas with their four children: Hazel, Ruth, George and Romagene. I never knew Rosa, my maternal grandmother, who died while giving birth to Romagene, who was four or five years older than I.

I have glaucoma, and it is likely that some of my ancestors had it. I have heard of no blindness or insanity in my family. People who read this paper may question the "insanity" ingredient.

I married Lottie Balk on May 31, 1945, while we were both in the Marine Corps. Lottie was born in Hoboken, New Jersey. We have three children: Ronald, Clifford and Celia (Bunny). Ronald has a daughter Lisy who is married to Leonard McKennon and they have a daughter,

Audrey, and a son, Edward. Bunny is married to Stephen Lee and they have two daughters, Emily and Anna Caroline.

Lottie's father was born in Lithuania and her mother was born in Poland. They spoke mostly Yiddish and some broken English. Lottie's background is much more interesting than mine and I wish she would record some of her memories.

Chapter 3:
Boyhood Experiences on Farm

I was born on a 40-acre hill farm in the Mt. Zion community, seven miles north of Piggott, Arkansas, three and a half miles west of St. Francis, and three miles east of Pollard. My sisters, Madeline and Mildred, were age three and two when I was born and Madeline remembers some of the things surrounding my birth. We did not have a phone and Grandma Brown lived about a mile and a half away from us. On his way to Piggott to fetch a doctor, dad stopped to tell his mother that I was birthing and he proceeded by horseback to get the doctor. Grandma came to our house and boiled water and found rags, and mid-wifed my birth. When grandma started to work with mom, she put Madeline and Mildred on the step outside the kitchen door and when they heard mom screaming with pain they ran back into the house, and grandma grabbed one under each arm and put them back outside. We never had a door that locked. Madeline says about all she can remember is there was blood everywhere, bloody rags and blood on grandma's apron.

Mt. Zion Methodist Church was located about one-half mile from us as the crow flies, but we usually went in a mule-drawn wagon and it was a mile around the road. People attended the closest church. Convenience, not religious dogma, dictated denomination. Dad was the church leader. He led the singing and said the prayers and, if the preacher, a circuit rider on a horse, didn't show up, dad gave the devotional and called on various members to give testimonials. Mom was very quiet and shy and never said a word or opened her mouth in church. Dad had an eighth grade education and I believe mom went to the third grade. About ten families attended Mt. Zion and all came in mule- or horse-drawn buggies or wagons. When church was over, about half the people went to the other half's house for Sunday dinner. The next Sunday, the process would be repeated except people went to different houses. Everyone had cows for milk and butter, chickens to eat and lay eggs, big vegetable gardens, a potato patch, and hogs to butcher for meat. The only things we had to buy were flour, sugar, salt and sometimes corn meal, but some times we took corn to a grist mill and had it ground into meal.

A typical breakfast was biscuits and gravy, fried pork, fried potatoes, and butter with sorghum molasses poured over it mixed with your knife and ladled onto a hot biscuit. On special occasions, we also had eggs and fried chicken–two generations of fowl at the same meal! We churned our own butter until we broke the churn, and then we used a half-gallon mason glass jar filled about half full of cream. We shook it until the butter separated from the whey, and then molded the butter into a ball.

The slop (hog feed) consisted of dirty dish water which mom saved in a big bucket. We stirred in three or four scoops of shorts (finely ground wheat) or chops (ground corn) and poured that mixture into a trough which extended about 12 or 18 inches beyond the fence which confined the hogs. The hogs would try to root each other away, climb over each other and grunt and squeal. The reason for the extension of the trough through the fence was to make it unnecessary for the feeder to get into the hog pen while feeding the hogs. If given the opportunity, the hogs pushed and rooted, and tried to drink out of the bucket and knock you down and spill the slop all over the ground. When a pig was about two months old, we castrated the males and dad slapped a handful of salt or doused some kerosene in the wound. We would also ring their noses, so their noses were too sore to root the ground up and escape under the fence.

Most of the churches and schools had outside toilets called "privies." Mt. Zion had no privy. The men went behind the church to relieve themselves. If a woman or girl had to go, she got someone to stand guard. Sometimes the men used a nearby barn or shed at the churches when they answered the call of nature.

At Christmas time we always had a Christmas tree at church (never at home), a children's program, singing of Christmas songs and, near the end of the service, Santa Claus came bursting through the door yelling, "Merry Christmas" loud enough to scare all the little ones who ran to their mommies. Santa had a small paper bag of goodies and a little present for every kid, and that was unforgettable!

At the Sunday dinners, the men and children ate at the first table and then, when the weather was warm, the kids went out and played in the yard, and the men folks sat on the porch and talked about their crops and livestock, while the ladies ate and washed the dishes and gossiped for a while. No prior arrangements were made about visiting before we went to church; thus mom never knew if we would be going to someone else's house for dinner, or if she would be feeding ten to twenty people. If people came to our house, she just fried more pork, opened another half gallon of green beans, made more cornbread or biscuits, fried or mashed more potatoes, and opened another half gallon of canned fruit. Every year we canned many quarts and half-gallons of fruits and vegetables.

We did not have a well on our farm, only a cistern. Wells are dug deep enough to tap into an underground stream of water and would therefore be a source of water year round. Cisterns are rainwater receptacles, dug about 15 to 20 feet deep, with a radius of about six feet, with concrete bottom and sides. Troughs around the eaves of our house collected the rain water and funneled it into the cistern. When we drew water from the cistern, there was a bucket tied on a rope, and a pulley. We had to be careful to keep the cistern covered in order to keep the dogs and cats and kids and varmints from falling into it, because it was a big problem when the water supply was fouled. During droughts, the cistern and ponds, from which the livestock drank, ran dry, so we had to haul water about one mile for our household use, and for the livestock, from a neighbor's deep-well, which had a pump that had to be "primed" before the water would come out.

Lest the buckets used to draw deep-well water are no longer made when my great-great-grandchildren read this, I will describe them. They are cylindrical in shape, with about a four-inch radius, and about three feet long. They are made of metal and have a valve attached to a slim metal rod which has a loop at the top. When you lower the bucket into the well, the force of the water opens the valve, and you can hear it bubble when it's filled. Then, when the bucket is drawn out of the water, the weight of the water inside the bucket forces the valve back down. When you get it to the top, you can either put your finger through the loop and let the water out the bottom, or pour the water out into another container.

The drought season was usually in the summertime, and the wooden shingles on the roof became covered with dust, which was washed into the cistern when the rains came. Almost every summer we used almost all of the water in the cistern, leaving a layer of mud on the bottom of the cistern, usually around ten to twelve inches deep. When the water was low, the water bucket contained some of the mud, and the water started looking brown and dirty, when it was drawn. That was when we hauled water from a neighbor's deep-well, and cleaned out the cistern. Since I was the smallest one, dad told me to hold on to the water bucket and, by use of a rope and pulley, he lowered me to the bottom of the cistern. I then filled the bucket with muddy water and dad drew it up. I then did the same thing with the mud, and when the floor of the cistern was as clean as I could get it, he drew me back up. When the rains started, the cistern was ready to receive the rainwater again.

Since we didn't have electricity, we had no way to keep food cold, so in order to keep the butter from spoiling, mom put it, and maybe two or three other perishable items, in the water bucket, and lowered the bucket down into the cistern just above the water level, and, thus, the food was kept cool enough to prevent spoiling. When we hauled water, we used big 50-gallon metal drums, loaded into a wagon, drawn by mules. The wagon wheels were made of wooden spokes with an iron rim on the outside, which rolled on the ground. In the summertime, during the drought, the iron rims expanded or the wood shrank. At any rate, I know that before we drove to the deep-well, we had to back the wagon with all four wheels into a pond so that wooden part of the wheels expanded enough to keep the iron rims from falling off.

It isn't that my great-great-grandchildren couldn't live full, productive lives without that bit of information. I guess the reason I've added it, is to show my quirky mind. In case some of those quirky genes make it down three or four generations, that might help them understand something about themselves.

Chapter 4:
Education

Education was not a major force in our lives. We lived about one mile from Starr School, as the crow flies, and we walked to school when we could cross a creek. In bad weather dad drove a wagon pulled by a team of mules, and took us and the neighbor kids to school, and came and got us when school was out in the afternoon. It was about two miles around the road, and only mail routes had gravel and bridges. When it snowed, dad came and got us in a sled that was drawn by a team of horses, and we really enjoyed that. I loved to smell the sweaty horses when it rained or snowed.

Starr School was a one-room school for grades one through eight with, maybe, 20 to 25 kids ranging in age from six to 17 years. Most dropped out before the eighth grade. The teacher's desk was in the front center of the room, facing the kids, who sat on wooden, fold-down seats attached to a desk which had a shelf for books and school supplies, two kids per desk. The bigger kids sat in the back of the room. When the teacher said it was time for fourth grade reading, the fourth graders walked to the front of the room and sat on the front row of seats, and read aloud until the teacher called the next group, for example, seventh grade arithmetic or sixth grade spelling, etc.

Teachers usually had pets and let them go to the well house and draw a fresh bucket of water before each recess at mid-morning and mid-afternoon. All of us drank from the same cup, which was called a gourd dipper. There was an outhouse for boys and one for girls, but no place to wash your hands. We played outside at recess, unless it was raining. We ran foot races, played "Wolfie over the River" (a form of tag), marbles, hopscotch, etc. The teacher rang a bell to end the recess. The period which was not recess was called "books." The teacher told her pet, "time for books," and the pet rang the bell and the kids ran in and sat in their assigned seats. We had split terms. School started in late summer and continued until the cotton was ready to pick, and then recessed for six weeks until the cotton was picked. On dark, cloudy, days we had a coal-oil (kerosene) lamp or lantern hanging on the wall or sitting on the teacher's desk. We had a wood-burning stove in the corner for heat in the winter. There was no grass on the school yard, just hard clay dirt. We had no homework because we had no lights at home other than a coal-oil lamp. On Friday afternoons, we had spelling bees. I don't recall that we had tests and I don't recall that we had report cards. Kids just automatically passed to the next grade. The teacher was always a female and had no college degree. We had no library. I don't remember how I or we decided that I was smart enough to be high school material. I believe that Madeline and Mildred finished the eighth grade, but neither of them attended high school. During WWII, teachers were so scarce that Mildred got a certificate that authorized her to teach in grade school, I think at Nimmons.

Chapter 5:
Boyhood Home

Our house had three rooms: front and middle rooms, about 20 feet square (the two rooms ran north and south), with a smaller kitchen jutting to the east from the middle room. In the front room were a wood-burning stove, called a king heater, mom and dad's bed, two or three cane-bottom rocking chairs and three or four straight-back chairs. When needed, the bed was used to sit on. I believe there was also a chest of drawers in the front room, as we called it. Mom and dad and the baby slept in the front room. The middle room had two double beds but no heat (there must have been only one double bed at first because I remember that Madeline, Mildred and I slept in the same bed for awhile). There was a big trunk for storage at the foot of the bed and a big quilt box along the south wall. Both the front room and the middle room had nails driven into the walls where we hung our clothes, because we had no clothes closet. There was a window in the west wall and a door on the back porch in the west wall (boys and men would pee off the back porch at night and I remember there was always a bad odor). Girls used what we called a "slop jar," which was a chamber pot. There was a door in the east wall of the middle room that led to the kitchen, which had a wood-burning cook stove and a large rectangular table with a wooden bench which seated about four or five people along the east side of the table, next to the cook stove. Sugar, salt, pepper, vinegar, molasses, butter, opened jars of fruit, jelly and vegetables were left on the tabled, covered with a table cloth to keep the flies off.

When Reba was born in 1926, she slept with mom and dad in the front room for a few years. Then we got a second double bed in the middle room and Reba and I slept in it for a few years. Dad was not much of a carpenter, but Uncle Earl, Uncle Raymond and Uncle George helped dad build an "ante" room on the west side of the house. A door entered off the back porch into a small room which had no ceiling, just a slanted roof, too low for a grown person to stand erect on the low slant, with clothes hanging from nails on the west wall, and a double bed along the east wall. Mom and dad slept in that bed during warm weather. All the beds had feather beds (duck or goose down) which we used in cold weather.

Probably because there was not much else to do, teenaged farm boys were preoccupied with sex. Not so with the girls. I guess the mothers put the fear of God in them. In the one room school in which I attended, the big boys masturbated all the time. One funny scene I recall was a big raw-boned boy masturbating. The teacher saw him, and started walking rapidly toward him. He saw her coming, but he couldn't quit. He was too far gone and he was sitting there all red faced and humped up and breathing hard. She slapped him so hard that he fell onto the floor. The bigger girls tried to look away when such things went on.

When I was about nine or ten years old, the Mt. Zion Church needed painting. An itinerant painter drifted through the countryside and offered to paint the church for us, and dad offered him room and board. Probably because they did not want him sleeping in the same room with my sisters, the painter and I slept in the front room and he performed oral sex on me each of the two or three nights he stayed with us. Of course, I had no idea at that time what he was doing. I remember that it woke me up and I felt under the cover and his hairy head was in my crotch area. One of dad's farm helpers also performed oral sex on me a year or so later. My first heterosexual experience was when I was about 12 or 13. I rode a horse to a revival meeting at Chigger's Chapel and when the singing and shouting were taking place, a girl and I went outside and leaned up against my horse and we did something that was very exciting, I'm not sure exactly what, but there probably was no penetration.

Some members of my family have expressed their opinion that I should omit the "sex" stuff, and they may be right. But, it happened.

Even if it had no role in molding my persona, it may have some historical value in reflecting what it was like growing up on a farm in Arkansas in the early 20th century. No moral turpitude on my part is involved. I suspect that what took place then is mild, compared to what kids do today. For example, I was acquainted with only one person who was divorced. Today, about one-half of all marriages end in divorce with no stigma attached. Today, couples live together without benefit of clergy, with no stigma attached. Such was unheard of in the 1920s, and would have been considered shameful and intolerable.

Chapter 6:
Life on the Farm

Our 40-acre farm was red clay hills, with only about ten acres of fertile creek-bottom land. One hilltop was flat enough to grow cotton, perhaps two or three acres, and the bottom land we planted in corn for feed for the chickens and livestock. The rest of the farm was pasture land. We drove two or three miles to the "bottoms" and share-cropped more cotton and corn land. We usually had two teams of horses or mules. During planting, cultivating and harvest seasons, we got up early and did the chores in the dark by lantern light, while mom fixed breakfast and packed our dinner (biscuits, pork sandwiches, a jar of soup beans, several baked sweet potatoes and a jar of canned fruit). After breakfast, all of us drove to the bottoms. We tried to get there about daylight, and we worked until dark. We then went back home and did the chores in the dark while mom cooked supper, and then we went to bed. Our daily chores were: feed the chickens (about 100 hens), gather the eggs, slop the hogs, and milk the cows. Mom made all of her and the girls' clothing and we bought our overalls and shoes at the store. We had to sell the eggs and cream to have money to buy what mom could not make. We got to eat eggs only on Easter morning, and when we were sick or had birthdays.

We had a five-acre peach orchard, two June apple trees, two pear trees, two Stark apple trees, two Ben Davis, two Golden Delicious and two Wine Sap apple trees. We canned lots of fruits and vegetables and stored them in a cool storm cellar which we ran to every time it looked stormy. Dad was afraid of storms and the neighbors teased him, but we were afraid to enjoy the teasing. We had quilts on the dirt cellar floor and slept there most of the night when it was stormy. We had dirt shelves dug along the walls for canned food, fresh apples and potatoes which smelled awful when they started to rot. There were lots of toad frogs in the cellar but they were harmless.

We dried fresh apples every fall. They would be thin-sliced and spread on a sheet to allow them to dehydrate in the sunshine. They were kept in flour sacks for delicious dried apple pies, fried in lard. Also, dried peach pies.

Chapter 7:
Hog-Killing Time

We usually fattened about six hogs for meat, and killed them at the first cold spell. Two or three neighbors came early, and dad and the men killed the hogs with a .22 rifle or pole-ax (hit them in the forehead), then slashed the hog's throat to let all the blood drain out. The hog was then sloshed around in a slanted barrel about one-fourth full of scalding hot water to soften the hair enough that it could be scraped off with a sharp knife. The hog was hung by its hind legs on a rail, head down, nose almost touching the ground, and slit open from tail to the slashed throat. The entrails were pulled out. Some tenderloins and brains were cut out to fix for dinner, which everyone ate.

That afternoon, the men and the women cut the fat off the entrails, boiled the fat in a big iron kettle until the fat was a hot liquid, then poured it into 5-gallon tin cans (called stands) and, when it congealed, it became lard. We usually had enough lard to last all year to cook and season the food. The residue was called "cracklings" and mom used the cracklings to season cornbread. The rest of the hog was cut up into hams, shoulders and middlings. Portions were trimmed off and seasoned with salt, sage and pepper after it had been run through a hand-cranked sausage grinder. The hams and the shoulders were hung on wires above smoldering hickory sawdust in the smokehouse until it was cured and hickory-smoked. The boneless middlings were stacked and rubbed all around the edges with dry salt and stored in a wooden box with a lid, to be removed one at a time as we ate them during the year. Usually dry salted meat slices were fried for breakfast and served with fried potatoes, biscuits and gravy. The hams were for special occasions and the shoulders were for supper. We never had enough pork to last until the young roosters got big enough to fry in the spring, and when we ran out of fryers, we killed rabbits to eat until the next hog-killing time. We got meat-hungry every fall, and it didn't take much of a "norther" for dad to "shiver up" a hog-killing. Hog-killing day was very exciting. Dad would say to mom, "Hazel, I'm gonna round up Raymond and Edna, George and Kathleen and 'the mung hands of "uv 'em' and kill hogs today". (I guess the phrase in quotations was a corruption of "among all of us will kill hogs".) Nothing was wasted. After the fat was trimmed off the entrails (for lard rendering), we fed the entrails to the hogs. Chickens and hogs are nasty. They will eat anything. Their meat could not have been very healthful.

When we ran out of pork in late summer, we went hunting for rabbits. We worked until late afternoon until the rabbits started foraging, about one hour before dark, in the cool evening. We hunted fence rows, creek beds and woods. I remember one year some of our pork spoiled and we ran out of meat early. The fried chicken season had been over a couple of months and we were starving for meat. The rabbits were scarce that year, too. It was getting too dark for dad to see how to shoot a rabbit and he said to me, with his voice trembling, "Son, it looks like ye mammy ain't gonna have no meat on the table again tonight." That's one of the saddest moments I remember and I am crying even now as I dictate this.

Chapter 8:
Crop-Planting Time

In the early spring, usually around March, we began preparing the soil for planting by burning off dead vegetation, and cutting the persimmon and sassafras sprouts that had grown up since the last year. We used a stalk cutter to chop the dead corn and cotton stalks from the year before. After the corn was harvested, we usually turned in the cows and horses so they could forage in the field. Next, we disked the cotton and corn rows to level them with the middles. The disking further chopped the cotton and corn stalks into pieces small enough that they would decay faster.

Next came the breaking plow which would "turn it under," that is, it flipped the top eight to 12 inches of soil. Breaking ground was very slow work. You could turn over only about a 12-inch wide strip at a time. The off mule walked in the furrow (pronounced "furry") about 12 inches deep, and the lead mule walked on the unplowed soil, so the off mule was about 12 inches lower than the lead mule. You plowed in rectangles, starting on the outside edge of the field, and made a 90-degree left turn when you reached the end of the unplowed ground. It was pretty tricky to hold the plow handles evenly and cut square corners. The first time I tried to manage it by myself (age nine or ten), I was so nervous and got so tired that it made me sick. Four or five acres a day is all you can turn. If you lift the plow handles, it plows too deep and the mules get too hot and tired. The broken ground is then disked, to crumble the big chunks of soil into little pieces. Then you harrow (we pronounced it "har") it to break it up into smaller clods.

For cotton, we used a lister to throw the soil up in rows about ten to 12 inches high, then harred or dragged the rows to smooth them. Then a mule-pulled cotton planter was used to plant one row at a time, dropping the cotton seed about every four to six inches, two or three inches deep. After the baby cotton plant came up, we used a scraper to scrape the grass and weeds away from the baby cotton, and we chopped the area between the baby cotton plants with a hoe. When corn is planted, the harrowing is followed by a drill (planter) which plants the seeds about 12 to 15 inches apart and about two to three inches deep (we did not plant corn on top of a ridge). We cultivated cotton and corn with horse-drawn implements which loosened the soil and destroyed weeds and grass. The number of times you had to chop and plow depended upon the amount of rain.

We tried to lay the crop by (finish with the chopping and plowing) by July 4th and then go to the picnic in Piggott and, maybe, go fishing (seining, in the nearest river or ditch). We seined with a net which we dragged along the muddy bottom and trapped fish; we then disentangled the flopping fish from the net, usually getting finned in the process.

When we cleared the trees and brush off an area, the cleared area was called "new ground," and it had to be plowed with a horse-drawn single shovel or double shovel rather than a breaking plow because the soil is laced with roots. When part of the shovel hit a big root, the nose of the plow dipped, and the handled jerked up, catching you in the groin, or it peeled the root and bent it and, when it cleared the shovel, it whacked you on the shin. It was very difficult to cultivate new ground for the first two or three years, but the soil was so fertile that a poor stand of corn yielded a decent crop.

Chapter 9:
Between Crop Plantin' and Harvest

After the crops were laid by and before we started harvesting in the fall, we mended fences, cleaned out fence rows, hauled the accumulated manure from the horse stables and cow barn, and scattered it on the fields as fertilizer. The manure from the chicken house fertilized the potato patch and the vegetable garden. We never had grass on our yard. The chickens kept it eaten off as soon as it peeked through the soil. In fact, we cleaned our yard with a broom and we swept the chicken droppings off the porch regularly. Mom threw the kitchen waste to the chickens and they came running when they heard her scrape a plate or pan.

Milking was a pleasure after the cow stables were cleaned; you did not have to wade the muck up to your knees. My sisters and I did the milking, and I squirted milk on them if dad was not close by. We put kicking chains on the cows that kicked. While you are milking, the cow would switch her tail and hit you in the face, and if the bushy end of her tail had cockle (kukkel) burs, it hurt your face. In the spring when grass was plentiful, the cows had calves and came "fresh," which means they had large udders for milk. We let the baby calves suck the mother cow for four or five days, then weaned the calf and taught it to drink skim milk, after we ran it through the cream separator, which was hand-cranked. We sold the cream, and fed the milk to the calves and the hogs. The cows ate the afterbirth (placenta) and the sows did also, and licked the babies until they were clean and dry. As soon as the calf could stand alone and could find its mother's teats, it started sucking. When calves suck, they hunch (a sudden, hard upward thrust of the head) and when you are feeding them from a bucket, you immerse your hand in the skim milk and let one finger stick up and they suck on that finger until they drink the milk. When they hunch, it scares you, hurts your finger, splashes the milk everywhere and usually turns the bucket over, and is very aggravating.

We fed corn to the horses, hogs and chickens, and all of the livestock drank water from ponds until they ran dry. We cut hay every fall. Dad did the mowing and I did the raking with a bull rake. The rake had two large wheels and was pulled by two mules. The wheels had gears in the housing on each wheel. When I hit the tripper with my foot, a hook caught in the gear and quickly raised the curved teeth which collected the hay and raked it into windrows. We then drove a wagon with a hay frame on it along the windrows and used a pitchfork to pile the hay on the wagon. We hauled it to the barn and pitched it into the hay loft. This was very hard work, especially if the hay was too green. After the hay was cut it was important to get it into the barn before it rained. Otherwise, it would get dirty and dusty and cause the horses to get distemper (I suppose, a form of pneumonia). Also, green hay would mildew and cause animals' sickness. Hay work was easier after we had a hay fork installed in our barn. A wooden track ran from the front of the barn to the back (a distance of about 50 or 60 feet, along the peak of the pitched roof). A large two-pronged iron fork on a rope and pulleys lifted the hay from the wagon. A mule at the other end of the barn pulled the rope which was attached to the fork at the front of the barn, and lifted the loaded hay fork up to the track where it rode along the track on rollers until it reached the point in the hay loft where the hay was to be stored. The person in the loft yanked a trip rope and the hay dropped, and, at that point, the mule pulling the hay turned around and went back to the barn. When the fork full of hay was being lifted vertically from the wagon to the track, a distance of some 20 to 30 feet, the mule had to pull very hard to lift it. The man on the wagon pulled the hay fork back to the wagon and loaded it again. Some farmers had hay balers. The hay was baled in the field where it grew. They hauled the hay from the windrows to the baler where it was compressed into rectangular bales about six feet long, weighing about 50 pounds, and then hauled to the barn and stacked. That was much easier and neater and also easier to flake off and feed to the livestock.

Farmers usually swapped work when putting up hay but not so with cotton picking and corn gathering. The helpers were paid by the pound for cotton picking and so much per day for gathering corn. A load of cotton weighed about 1500 pounds (three sideboards high on the wagon) and ginned out to about a 500-pound bale. The closest cotton gin was in St. Francis, about three and a half miles away from our house, but not that far from our share-cropped lands in the bottoms. If dad thought he could get a better price at the gin in Piggott, we took it there, seven miles. When we got to the gin, there was a line of loaded cotton wagons waiting to pull under the suck. While waiting our turn, dad sent me to the store to buy ten cents worth of bologna and crackers for our lunch. When our turn came to unload, dad could push and pull the suck around our load fast enough to finish unloading it in about 20 minutes. We drove the loaded wagon across the scales, and then the empty wagon, and then dad went inside and to settle up. We then drove by the store and dad bought some candy, cheese or bologna (all delicacies) for mom and the girls. It would be dark when we got home, but they were there waiting expectantly for their treats.

The corn gathering usually had to wait until the cotton was picked because the shucks protected the grain from the weather. It took three people to gather the corn, five rows at a time. The mules, which were muzzled to keep them from eating corn, pulled the wagon down the middle row, which was called the down row. Mom gathered the two rows on one side of the down row, and dad the two rows on the other side. I picked up the corn from the down row off the ground. We threw the ears of corn into the wagon. When it got full, we hauled it to the corn crib and took turns shoveling it into the crib. The shuck stayed on the ear of corn, so as we fed it, we had to shuck it, feeding the shucks to the cows and the ears of corn to the horses, hogs and chickens. If it looked like the crops were puny, we cut the stalks of corn for feed. We shocked it (stood them up in clusters and tied wire around them), and fed them to the cows and horses as a fodder - not as nutritious as hay and corn.

Chapter 10:
Nobody Here But Us Chickens

We had nests built in the hen house for the hens to lay eggs in. We put sticks in one part of the hen house for them to roost on (stand on while they were sleeping), the sticks being small enough for them to wrap their toes around while they slept. The roosts were about three feet high. Chickens have mites (tiny parasites too small to see) and when we crawled under the roosts to clean out the droppings, we always got mites on us - a nasty, miserable, stinky job. When the weather got warm, the hens laid their eggs outside in fence rows, peach orchards, cow pastures, anywhere they could find vegetation. When we gathered up the eggs, we had to look not only in the nests in the hen house, but all around. We knew about how many eggs there should be so we just kept looking until it got dark or until we thought we had found them all. Chickens can fly up into the trees with low limbs to sleep at night and predatory wild animals would kill them. We tried to fence the chickens in and clipped one of their wings so they could not fly over the fence. One time my dad thought someone was stealing our hens. Our hound dog, Old Blue, started barking in the middle of the night, and dad took a loaded double-barreled shotgun to investigate. Dad slept in his long underwear which had a trap door (flap) in the seat. When dad leaned inside the hen house, trying to find the thief, Old Blue stuck his cold nose into the trap door, touching dad's bare bottom. Dad screamed and squeezed the trigger, killing several hens.

Chickens go to roost at dusk, so as the cold weather approached, we tried to break their tree habit and forced them back into the hen house. If we did not get home before dark, the chickens missed their supper. It was fun to feed the chickens, because when they saw you walking toward the feeding block, they came running and swarmed you, and flew up into the bucket where the food was while you tried to feed them. In the spring, you could take an ear of corn and entice a fryer to come close enough to grab him; then wring his neck until his head came off in your hand. When he quit flopping, you knew he was dead. You then dipped him into hot water until you could pluck the feathers. Sometimes, instead of wringing their heads off, we put his head under a broom handle, and stood with one foot on either side of his head and pulled up on his legs until his head came off. We didn't kill the pullets because we needed them to grow into egg-laying hens. You could tell the pullets from the males because the males had larger and redder combs. We spared two or three roosters for breeding purposes so the eggs would be fertile and hatch baby chicks. When the laying cycle was ending, the settin' hen sat on the nest with about 12 eggs in it, night and day except long enough to eat and drink, until the eggs hatched. We loved to watch the baby chick peck its way out of the egg shell. Each mother hen would hatch eight or ten baby chicks and they were her flock. They followed her around, and she showed them how to forage for themselves, and, when she clucked, they ran to her. Maybe six weeks to two months later, the mother hen cut the strings and drove the chicks away. When the baby chicks were young they slept at night under the mother's wings. She squatted near the ground and, as darkness came, the chicks crawled under her wings. She would cluck to them and talk them into bed. Sometimes an unruly chick would balk and she would scold it with a harsh cluck. When they had all crawled under her wings, she lowered her body and hovered over them until daylight. If the chicks depended on her to find their food too long, she pecked them to drive them away.

It was routine for farm kids to see pigs and calves and dogs and cats being born. Sometimes dad would have to pull the calf from the cow's behind when it got cross-ways. One time, our city cousin, Tom, was visiting us. When dad was pulling the calf, Tom said, "wonder how fast that calf was running when it hit the cow." Normally, the front feet and the head of the calf would appear first.

We put a forked tree limb, called a yoke, on the cows which had the habit of escaping from their pasture. The yoke would get caught up in the fence. When the cows got out, that was an emergency. Everyone ran to round them up and herd them back into the field and fix the fence where they got out. If they broke out when we were not at home, they could ruin a corn field and eat so much corn that they would founder and die. Grandpa Brown had a fatal heart attack while he was trying to get his bull back into the pasture. When cows were in heat, bulls could smell it and jump fences and fight each other to get to the cow. We did not keep a bull (too much trouble), so when our cows came into heat, we led or hauled them to the closest bull for breeding purposes. The owner of a pedigreed bull charged a stud fee. We never used such an exalted bull, so we didn't have to pay. The bull's pleasure was sufficient compensation. When the calf was born, the milk cycle started again, usually in the spring. Milk and eggs were in short supply in the winter time.

Chapter 11:
Pleasure and Hygiene

Saturday was trade day. We loaded our eggs and cream into the wagon and drove to town and sell our stuff and buy the things we needed, and to visit with other farm families while in town. Kids went to a western movie and, maybe, get a hot dog or popcorn. We would spend the day and get home in time to do chores while mom cooked supper.

Saturday night was bath night, in a No. 3 wash tub. All of us bathed in the same water. Our cook stove was in the kitchen and the heating stove was in the front room. If the kitchen was warm, we bathed there. Mom heated a dishpan full of water and poured it in the tub, adding enough cold water to get it lukewarm. Mom made our soap, using lye and water, and something to make it congeal, probably a by-product of lard or grease. She cut the soap into three-inch squares and that was what we used for dishwashing, hand washing and bathing. The girls bathed first, then me, then dad and mom. We had to bathe fast so the water wouldn't get too cold for the others. All three rooms had linoleum floor covering so it was easy to mop up spilled water. When it was too cold to take a tub bath, we used a small wash pan of water and a wash rag. The joke was that we washed up as far as possible, and then down as far as possible, then wash "possible." We used the same wash pan to wash our hands and face, and used the same towel, made from flour sacks. Babies' aprons (dresses) were also made from flour sacks. We all drank water from the same bucket and used the same dipper. When water was scarce we gave the dirty bath water to the chickens and hogs.

In the winter, when our heels, elbows, knees and backs of our hands became chapped, we rubbed glycerin on them. We used kerosene as first aid for cuts and scratches, and Vick's salve on a flannel rag pinned to our undershirt for colds.

There was always a nearby creek that had swimming holes. In the summer time, we went swimming in the nude. Boys would find a swimming hole every Sunday and spend most of the afternoon there. If the girls found their own swimming hole, the boys tried to sneak close enough to see them in their underwear. Some times we grabbed their dresses, which they had left on the creek bank, and run off with them. We teased the girls and pretended that we would not return the dresses, but, finally, we put the dresses back because we feared the consequences if they went home and told the parents we had been spying on them. A "whupping" would certainly result. Before we returned their dresses, we made them promise not to tell on us. The swimming holes usually had muddy water but that didn't bother us.

If we got behind with our farming on account of the weather, we might have to forego our trip to town on Saturday, but we never worked on Sunday - a cardinal sin. Farm families always attended the nearest church. Every summer churches in the area would have week-long revivals, usually under a brush arbor, and we might drive two or three miles for a revival. A visiting evangelist preached fire and brimstone and hell and eternal damnation to all who were not saved. At the end of every service, the congregation sang songs like "Why Not Tonight?" and the preacher urged sinners to come to the mourner's bench (front seat of the church). He or she sat down on the mourner's bench and family members knelt around and prayed long and loud. After a few minutes the sinner suddenly jumped up and started grabbing outstretched hands proclaiming acceptance of Christ as his savior. Friends and relatives shouted "hallelujah," and jumped up and down and bounced all around the church, some speaking in unknown tongues and frothing at the mouth. My Grandma Brown who was a large, fat woman, was a great shouter. The night my Uncle Connie was saved at a revial in a brush arbor, she bounced so high, while shouting, that her head hit a knot where a limb had been cut off, and it knocked her out cold. Some churches featured such entertaining shouters, people came from miles around. There were some hard-hearted sinners who went to the mourner's bench night after night and year after year, but never got saved. On the other hand, there were the back-sliders who got saved every revival. I remember the night I got saved. While Grandma Brown was shouting, my taciturn Uncle Carl, who seldom said a word, solemnly walked up to me, shook my hand, and let out a "Praise the Lord." When the revival was over, all of the converts were hauled to the St. Francis River where the preacher led us all, holding hands, into the water (about waist deep), and baptized us one Sunday afternoon.

Uncle Carl was the family barber. He had scissors and a pair of clippers that were dull. When he started up the back of your neck it would hurt like the devil. He called the crevice in the back of your neck a "schoolhouse." He worked for free so we didn't complain except to flinch when it pulled. To minimize the pain, I squeezed by neck back, and he called me "no neck."

Mom made patchwork quilts every winter. Sometimes neighbor women came to quilt and visit, all afternoon. Mom sewed all of her own and the girls' clothing, and she made our shirts and underwear, but not overalls.

Our inside winter games were Authors (made with homemade square cards which were numbered). You asked for everybody's nines and they had to give you all their nines. When you got four cards with the same number you laid them down and had a book. Whoever had the most books at the end of the game was the winner. We also played Hide-the-Thimble, Spin-the-Top, and marbles. Outside games were Annie Over (throw a twine ball over the house, and if a kid on the other side of the house caught it before it hit the ground, he'd sneak around the corner of the house and hit you with the ball). We played horse shoes and washers, which we pitched at three small holes dug in the ground, the nearest hole was five points, the middle hole ten points, and the rear hole 15 points. On Sunday afternoons big boys and young men rode cows and bulls until they got bucked off. It was considered sinful to have a deck of cards in the house. We did have dominos and checkers in later years. We made a ball about the size of a baseball out of twine. There was a cow pasture nearby that had a flat area big enough to lay out a baseball diamond of sorts. For bases we used a tow sack filled with dirt, and a shovel handle for a bat. Most of us knew that when the batter hit the ball he was suppose to run around the bases, but this one hick, who talked so slowly that he put you to sleep, did not know much about the game. One time he hit the ball over the fence and just stood there and watched it, and when his teammates yelled for him to run, he drawled, "I ain't running - I ain't no coward, I'll just pay for the damn ball."

Mom washed our clothing and bed sheets in a No. 3 wash tub, on a rub board (a wooden and tin contraption with corrugated ridges) with lye soap, which was hard on your hands. In fact, if you kept your hands in lye water too long, the lye would eat holes in your hands. You soaked the dirty clothes in hot lye water a few minutes to loosen the dirt, and then let the water get cool enough that you could put your hands in it. Then you put the rub board in the tub, which was setting on a bench about two feet high, and rub the clothes up and down the rub board ridges until the dirty spots came out. Then wring them dry and shake the garment out and dip it into a dish pan full of clear water, then in a pan with "bluing" to whiten the clothes. We called it "wrenching" but, of course, that really meant that we were rinsing the clothes to get the lye out. Otherwise the lye would irritate your skin and make your crotch itch and sting and be painful and embarrassing. After "wrenching," we hung them on wire clothes line strung between posts about 30 feet apart. The rubbing was hardest and we took turns with that. The rinsing was easy. You carried the clean clothes and sheets and wooden clothes pins to the clothes line. You set the pan of clothes on the ground, shake out the garment, holding a couple of clothes pins in your mouth, and then pin the garment to the clothes line. When the line (wire) was loaded with damp clothes, it sagged so much the clothes would reach the ground, so we had a stick to prop up the line about half way between the poles. In windy weather the clothing had to be pinned securely to keep them from blowing away. In cold weather the damp sheets and clothes might freeze stiff before you got them pinned on the line. Mom was reluctant to leave home with clothes on the line for fear that a strong wind would come up and blow them off the line, and we would find them blown against the fences, rose bushes, and so forth, so dirty they would have to be washed again.

When the weather got warm in the spring, the kids shed their shoes. It felt so good to get rid of the stiff heavy old brogans we wore in the winter time. I used to love to run and jump barefoot in the fresh plowed ground. I felt so light that I could jump a mile. I still have dreams about it. In my dreams I run so fast that I leave the ground and when I feel like I'm about to land again, I draw my legs up and glide another 100 feet or so and, sometimes, another quarter mile. Most of the time we had Sunday shoes for church and when we were about to outgrow them, we would start wearing them every day.

One morning I was on my way to the cow pasture to round up the cows and herd them into the barn so we could milk them. I was running barefoot in the dewy grass and stepped on a snake and was nearly scared to death. I've been afraid of snakes ever since. When snakes appear on TV, I close my eyes until someone tells me that it is safe. In late summer and early fall when I started to round up the cows, I'd stop by the apple orchard and get two or three Red Delicious apples to eat on my shepherding journey.

The bridles we used on our horses and mules had blinds to keep them from seeing behind, only front vision. We did not have saddles. A rope was used for a rein. When I was in grade school, we had a gray mare named Mart. When I got big enough to ride her, she was very gentle, and I claimed her as mine. I was so proud. I would run home from school and bridle her and jump on her back and gallop her a half mile to the mail route. Six or eight of the kids walked home from school and I would get there in time to show off to my "girlfriend." My best friend was Daniel Pillow and we frequently spent the night with each other. When I asked mom if I could spend the night with Daniel, she would say, "Law, child, I dunno. Ast yer daddy." When I was at his house, his sister, Alberta, would spend the night with my sisters. I was a bed wetter until my teens. When I spent the night at Daniel's, I did not drink any liquids that afternoon or evening, but sometimes I wet the bed anyway and be so embarrassed. The feather bed smelled of urine and Mr. Pillow would carry it out into the yard to let the sun dry it, leaving an ugly stain and terrible odor. My feather bed at home was in awful shape. Poor mom.

One of our cranky neighbors always had a watermelon patch and we boys would raid it, and he would shoot his gun in the air. It was great sport to steal Uncle Pine's watermelons. His wife, Aunt Becky, was spooky mean, snaggle-toothed and scary. No one ever visited them. (All old people were called aunt and uncle.) Before Uncle Pine died, he had some kind of painful illness, probably gall stones or kidney stones, and it hurt so badly that we could hear his groans and yells for a quarter of a mile. There was a huge oak tree near his house, on the side of the road which ran in front of his house. A few days after he died, Daniel and I had stayed out rather late and Mr. Pillows, switch in hand, came looking for us. When he heard us coming, he hid behind the tree near Uncle Pine's house and began groaning like Uncle Pine did, and we got scared and started running. When he caught us, he gave us both a good whipping with the tree limb. Before Daniel and I could go out at night, we had to help Mr. Pillow or my dad with the chores and eat supper before we left. Whipping was routine and automatic for misconduct. Daniel, or any other visiting kid, had to mind my dad and I had to mind theirs. Mom never disciplined, she'd always threaten us saying, "If you do that again, I'm gonna tell your daddy and he'll whup your britches."

You didn't need any money when you went sparkin' (courting) because there was no store or place to spend money. We would go to some nearby church to try to spark some of the girls, and the boys from some other community would come to Mt. Zion Church to spark the girls there, with the mothers keeping close watch. When my sister, Madeline, was about 15 or 16 she married a boy from Wonders Home Church, a general Baptist church about two miles from where we lived. Late one day I was sitting in our corn crib shucking corn and I saw my two sisters and their friend, a girl whom I claimed as my girlfriend, walking toward the crib. My overalls were ragged and had holes in the knees and seat, and I was so ashamed for my girlfriend to see me so shabbily dressed that I piled the shucks up all around my legs to cover them. They told me Madeline was going to get married that night after preaching was over and they wanted me to go to the wedding at Wonders Home, but I didn't want to stand up and let my girlfriend see me, so I would not go. Neither did mom or dad attend. After the wedding, Madeline and husband went to his father's house, and Mildred and her girlfriend came to our house. Mom and dad and I went to bed at the usual time and didn't wait up to get a report from Mildred on the wedding. No other kin attended, although several lived within two or three miles. I guess Madeline and Elvin just decided that afternoon to get married that night. Two or three nights later we gave them the usual chivaree - clanging bells and making noises outside the house where they were staying. If the newlyweds didn't come out and invite the revelers in and treat them with candy, we'd carry plows, discs, and any other farm implements and pile it on the front porch. The candy was usually peppermint stick or cream candy sticks or perhaps horehound candy or homemade molasses candy.

The only booze I remember was home brew - fermented and distilled fruit juice, I think. My dad never made any but I had one black sheep uncle who did. In fact, he went to jail for moonshining and getting drunk. After Grandpa Brown gave up on him, dad bailed him out a couple times, but he never repaid dad, so dad quit too. My Uncle Denver was only four or five years older than I, and I loved to spend the night at Grandpa Brown's. One night after my grandparents had gone to bed, Denver and I slipped out of the house. Denver saddled his horse and I rode behind. We went to Uncle Connie's. It was a Saturday night and they were having a square dance. The windows were open, and the house was dimly lit with coal oil lamps. We slipped around and peaked into the windows. We could smell what smelled like soured peaches (Denver said it was moonshine), and could hear guitars strumming, and fiddling and singing, and could see dancing inside. In a side room we could see a man and a woman on the bed moaning and groaning, and we suspected they were not dancing. After Madeline and Elvin married, Denver took to drink and got into trouble a time or two. He raised a ruckus one night at Mt. Zion. I think he was drunk and Elvin hid his horse, claiming Denver was too drunk to ride. The bad feeling escalated and the following Sunday night Denver and Elvin got into a fist fight. They rolled into a nearby ditch and Elvin got on top of him and beat him up pretty badly. Grandma Brown felt I should have helped Denver and we became estranged and I really missed visiting them after that. That estrangement lasted for a few months and, when it reached the point where I couldn't stand it any longer, I walked to their house after school. When I arrived, they welcomed me and I was so relieved.

Shortly after Madeline and Elvin married, dad and I and Elvin and his dad cut down, with a crosscut saw, enough small trees to build a log cabin near Wonder's Home Church. After the trees were felled, we sawed and chopped off the limbs. We sawed the trees into logs, peeled the bark off the sides to flatten them, cut notches near the end of each log for corners, stacked the logs on top of each other, filled the spaces between the logs with mortar (sand, dirt, gravel and cement mixed with water), made shingles, and put on a shingle roof. Madeline and Elvin lived in that log cabin for awhile and then it stood empty for several years. Within the past few years I have found the site where the cabin formerly stood and identified some of the pieces of mortar.

In Grandpa Brown's hilly cow pasture were some gullies (red clay hill sides eroded by gully washer rains). There was a series of gullies, separated by ridges tall enough to make each gully seem isolated. A loud yell or whistle from one gully would echo and reverberate for several seconds. Sliding down the ridges was great fun, especially when we boys were at the bottom and could see up the girls' dresses. When we had family reunions at Grandpa Brown's house, there were many grandchildren and we set up boards on sawhorses to create a food table under the catalpa trees in Grandpa's yard. After church we drove the wagon to Grandpa's house. Everyone brought food and spread it along the table, Grandpa said a prayer, and we loaded our plates. All the women were good cooks but each had a reputation for a special dish. Mom's was vinegar pie (deep dish cobbler). Grandma Brown's was hot custard (served in a glass with an inch of meringue one top). You'd drink it and the meringue gave everyone a mustache which was not a pretty sight for men with mustaches. After dinner, a dozen or so of the grandkids would gravitate to the gullies, after we had changed from our Sunday clothes. After playing for a while, some of the bigger boys began having sexy thoughts and eventually exposed their private parts, and the bigger girls screamed and ran away. The boys coaxed, cajoled and dared the girls to let us see their bottoms, and eventually some of them did--a quick peek followed by a squeal--and ran away. I remember one Sunday, after the exposures and fleeing had resulted in a chase to another gully, only a female cousin and I were left alone in the gully. She was a very shy girl, and had not taken part in any of the frolics. She walked slowly toward me, stood directly in front of me, and without uttering one word, slowly raised the front of her dress to the waist, pulled out the elastic top of her bloomers and gave me a good view of her hairless crotch. Without a word I leaned forward, looked down into her bloomers, and straightened up. She let go of the elastic and it popped against her belly. She dropped her dress in front of her and turned and started walking slowly to the other kids. We were both totally unimpressed and hadn't a clue wherein the thrill was. Some of the bigger girls did have a nest of pubic hair and the bigger the nest, the more exciting the game was.

Mom's brother, George Parker, married Dicey, who died of diphtheria before I was old enough to remember. He then married Kathleen, whom I do remember. Uncle George liked to farm but Aunt Kathleen got bored and they sold their farm and went up North. He worked in the car factories until she got bored again. Then they came back to Arkansas and lived with relatives until Uncle George bought another farm and set up housekeeping. All of the kin thought it was awful the way Aunt Kathleen wooled him around. One time when they had just returned to Arkansas and had not yet bought another farm, Uncle Raymond and Aunt Edna were getting ready to go to church. They knew that Uncle George and Aunt Kathleen would be there, so Raymond cautioned Edna, "Don't be too friendly with George and Kat or they'll be moving in with us." Jokes like that were repeated over and over at all Sunday gatherings - ad nauseum. Sparkling conversation, n'est ce pas?

Chapter 12:
It's Raining Education

When I finished eighth grade (I guess I was 14), I wanted to go to high school and the closest one was in Piggott, seven miles away. I was not acquainted with anyone, except perhaps one of my school teachers, who had ever attended high school. I don't suppose my parents were either, and they did not think it was important for me to go. Moreover, they needed me to work on the farm and help support the family. Too, since we did not live in the Piggott school district, tuition was $4.00 a month which dad could not afford. I laid out of school a couple of years and kept pleading my case. I heard about a government program (FDR's NRA - National Recovery Act) whereby I could pick up scrap paper off the school yard for my tuition. Dad finally gave in and told me in the summer of 1936 that if we got a badly needed rain in time to break the drought and make a good crop that year, he'd let me ride one of his plow horses to Piggott High School that fall. It was getting late and the crops were withering from the heat and the drought, and things were looking bleak. Probably in August, a big black cloud came up in the southwest late one afternoon and it began thundering and lightning and the wind came up. I remember I was sitting on the side of the bed looking out the west window, hoping and praying that it would rain. When big raindrops started peppering down on our tin roof (which magnified the noise of the falling rain) I jumped up and down yelling, "It's raining education." I can't remember why I did not ride Old Mart but for some reason I rode Old Bronc, a not too tame bronco.

We got a used saddle from someone. Old Bronc bucked sometimes and keep bucking until she threw you off. I found a shortcut through some woods which I used some times. The mail route to Piggott was seven miles and the short cut was probably five or six miles. One time while going through the woods, a covey of quails was flushed out by our approach and when they suddenly took off, wings afluttering, it scared Old Bronc and she jumped so suddenly that my foot went through the stirrup as I was falling off. She dragged me about a quarter mile then, uncharacteristically, stopped and stood still enough for me to be able to extricate my foot from the stirrup and remount. That is when I knew that the Good Lord was protecting me from harm. We were acquainted with an old man who lived near Piggott High School and he had an old barn and let me keep Old Bronc there. Dad hauled some hay to Uncle Dan's barn for me to feed her. Pauline Pfieffer's father lived near Piggott High School and Uncle Dan's barn was just a couple of blocks from school. Pauline married Ernest Hemingway and I have since learned that Mr. Hemingway wrote part of <u>Farewell to Arms</u> only a stone's throw from where Old Bronc was munching on hay in 1936. The Pfieffer Home is now the historic Pfieffer-Hemingway Museum. 'Tis a shame that some of Old Bronc's hoof prints were not preserved for the museum. The spot where my high school stood is now the parking lot for the Pfieffer-Hemingway Museum.

In the dead of winter, when it was really too cold with snow and ice to ride Old Bronc, I had to miss a few days of school. I had an Uncle Zeb who was a drifter, called a hobo, from my mom's folks, who moved from Indiana (pronounced Indiani) and Uncle Zeb spent his time drifting back and forth between Clay County and Indiani. He had long snaggled teeth, rotted by tobacco juice, and probably tuberculosis, or some disease that made him cough and spit vile stuff. We dreaded his visits. He made the trip on foot so many times that he joked that he could, "Borry a cup of sugar anywhere along the route from Arkansas to Indiani" (presumably he would repay the sugar on his next trip). I think he was called a tramp. He would knock on someone's back door and ask for a handout - something to eat. That winter he had found an abandoned store building in Piggott about ten by twenty feet, about a quarter mile from Piggott High School. The building had a dirt floor and he nailed a tow sack over the opening where the door used to be and hung some tow sacks over the windows. I believe he could do carpenter work when he wanted to. When the weather got so bad I couldn't ride the horse, I stayed with Uncle Zeb. We slept on straw piled in one corner. He had a wood stove to heat and cook on. I could not go out for football because I could not practice after school (I had to go home and help with the chores), but I could run like a gazelle and loved to play tag football. When I stayed with Uncle Zeb, I was ashamed for anyone to see me enter or leave the store building so I played tag football until dark, and sneak in. I would peek out in the morning until the way was clear.

I made the highest grade in the freshmen class. I always wore bib overalls and the girls wouldn't have anything to do with me socially, but I tried to win their favor by helping them with their studies and grades. We had a system, an arrangement of seats in some classes that when you could answer a question the others ahead of you missed, you, "turned them down," and moved ahead of them. I usually had the front seat, but if one of the pretty girls worked her way up close, I missed the answer on purpose so she could move ahead of me. Then I would whisper the answer to her so she could stay in the front seat. I kept my favorite girl in front of me so long I thought she was starting to like me, but I never got up enough nerve to ask her for a date.

Uncle Zeb's consumption caused him to hock and spit so much that when he visited us, at every meal he would have a coughing spell and nearly ruin our appetites when he got up from the table, go out to the porch to spit, and we could hear him. It would nauseate us. I don't know why I didn't catch TB when I was living with him in his shack. I remember one night he had a partial stalk of bananas hanging from the rafter. They were overripe and he probably got them cheap. I loved bananas and we seldom had them at home. I ate thirteen bananas that night and got sick. We had no bathroom; we used a pot and threw it out the back of the store every day.

Chapter 13:
The Fains, The O'Dells, and The Fire (tentative title)

The tangles in our hair were called "rat's nests." "A rat must have slept in your hair last night." Big joke! To keep from getting the itch, we wore vile smelling asafetida on a string around our neck. When we got sick, we had to take castor oil or black draught purgatives. For a cold, mom would rub Vick's salve on a flannel cloth and pin it inside our underwear on our chest. At night we'd hold the cloth up to the king heater until it was as hot as we could stand.

The heater burned wood and would get red hot and very dangerous for kids to play near. We cut and hauled the stove wood and kept the pile in our yard. Every night one of us kids would carry wood from the pile in the yard and stack enough on the porch to last through the night. We always quarreled about whose turn it was. Dad put a big stick of wood in the stove just before he went to bed so it would have some fire to rekindle the next morning. Kindling was small chips of wood.

We lived in hilly country and everyone's house was on the top of a hill. Our closest neighbor was Preacher Fain and his wife, Stella. They lived about an eighth of a mile west of us. A quarter mile east of us lived Uncle Raymond and Aunt Edna. The Fains moved about 1933 and their daughter, Lucille, and her husband moved there from St. Louis. Lucille was too "fine and citified" for us. The Fain Farm was 80 acres, most of it fertile creek bottom land, and we rented it from the Fains. One time when dad and I were plowing the Fain land, we heard mom screaming and jumping up and down waving her arms, yelling that our house was on fire. We ran home and the flames were burning the wood shingles all around the kitchen chimney. I can't remember exactly how dad got on the top of the roof (we had no ladder), but I remember seeing him ripping the flaming shingles with his bare hands and flinging them into the yard while we were drawing buckets of water from the cistern as fast as we could. Somehow we managed to get the fire out before it burned the house down. I remember dad's hands were so tough and calloused that they didn't get burned very badly.

When the O'Dells moved to the Fain Farm, Alvin farmed the land and we had to drive about three miles to rent bottom land. That may have been one of the reasons dad didn't much like Alvin. Whenever we swapped work with Alvin, dad always felt he came out on the short end of the deal. Alvin had a Shetland pony and I loved to ride it. It was round and soft and fuzzy. When you hired out to work for the day, it was for one dollar a day, sun up to sun down. Pitching hay was considered heavy work. I'd work for Alvin for 50 cents a day if he would let me ride his pony, and dad thought I was getting cheated on that deal.

Dad got the notion that someone was stealing corn from our crib at night or sometime when we'd be gone from home. He rigged up a double-barrel 12 gauge shotgun inside our corn crib in such a manner that when it was hooked up, opening the crib door would pull the trigger and blast to kingdom come anyone in the doorway. We lived in fear that it would kill some of us if dad forgot to unhook it, but, fortunately, nothing like that ever happened. I believe that that was one of the reasons dad bought the 80-acre farm near Greenway in 1936 or '37.

Chapter 14:
Transportation - The Horseless Carriage

For a short while, probably around 1933 to '35, we had a Model T Ford. I did not get to drive it but I remember the mystery and thrill and wonderment of riding in a vehicle that was moving without being pulled by a team of mules. Riding in it may have inspired my "barefoot" dreams previously recounted. How on earth could a heavy metal car move on its own force? I now know it had something to do with combustion and cylinders but it is still a mystery to me. At that time it felt like I was gliding through the air just above the surface, like a snowmobile or vehicle that hovers just above the water. I think it was a '28 or '29 model open touring car, with leather and cellophane curtains that you buttoned on in the rain or in cold weather. It had three pedals on the floor, the left one the clutch, the middle one reverse, and the right one the brake. The spark lever was on the left side of the steering column and the accelerator was on the right. It was always an adventure to start the engine, hand-cranked, hand-choked. The spark lever and accelerator had to be coordinated just right while someone cranked it. Since we lived on top of a hill, we'd leave the car in a position where we could push it to the road and get it started down hill in case the crank failed to start it. Then the pushers would jump in, falling on top of one another, and away we'd fly until we came to a steep hill which the car couldn't quite climb on its own. Then everyone but the driver would jump out and push it over the top, then pile back in. We always tried to get up enough speed so the momentum would carry us over the top of the next hill, but the bridges or muddy spots in the hollers sometimes killed the momentum. Some times dad would let it roll back down the hill and make another run at it while the pushers stood on either side of the road about half way up the hill, ready to start pushing when needed. Only the mail routes were graveled. The dirt roads got so rutted and muddy that cars couldn't traverse them in winter. That was probably the main reason we didn't keep the car very long. Probably about 1932 we got a rubber-tired wagon and it was luxurious. The old wooden-wheeled wagon, with the iron rims, was very rough, even if you had a spring seat.

In the spring of 1934 or '35, I got pneumonia (probably started going barefoot too early) and had to stay in bed for two or three weeks. When I was able to be up and about again, I was amazed to see the greenery. The spring showers and sunshine had worked wonders in two or three weeks. That is one of God's wonders – the miracle and dependability of spring. I think God's greatest miracle is the making of a human baby - the complex and intricate make-up of the human body. When I recently learned that my potassium level is too high, it really made me realize how the best minds in the world have been trying for thousands of years to understand what God wrought in a few minutes. How can anyone doubt the existence of God? Only God can make a tree.

In 1936 or '37 dad sold our 40-acre hill farm in the Mt. Zion community and bought an 80-acre bottom farm near Greenway. It was three or four miles west of Piggott and one and a half miles northwest of Greenway. We moved in the spring of '37 and I finished by first year of high school, walking to Piggott High School. Our house was only a nine-iron distance from a big creek. We had been living there only a few days when the '37 flood overflowed the creek which we called Sand Creek, and inundated our farm and most of the adjoining land. In the middle of the night we could hear the water sloshing under our house and lapping up against the joists, and when the lightning flashed we could see nothing but water. Dad carried my brother Don, and mom, Mildred, Reba and I started wading knee-deep water and we walked about an eighth of a mile to Uncle Loosh Mayo's house (which was on higher ground) and stayed until the water receded. Only about ten acres of the farm lay on the east side of the creek. We had to cross (fjord) the creek to get to the other 70 acres. When we were working, we had to make sure we got across the creek before the water got up or we would be trapped.

Chapter 15:
High School

It was easy to walk to Piggott High School from Sand Creek. We still had no electricity but we did have a well, which represented a big improvement over the cistern. I managed to study enough to make good grades and was awarded a medal for the highest grades in freshman class (perhaps 100 students), but was ashamed to walk to the front of the room at the general assembly of the student body on Award's Day to claim my medal because of my bib overalls. I went to Greenway High School my last three years and didn't learn anything of an academic nature. I did, however, learn how to have fun. I played basketball, played pool, and drank beer. The teachers were grandmotherly, who knew little about the subjects they were supposed to teach. I learned enough that one year at Piggott High School to coast through Greenway High School.

Two farm neighbor boys and I ran around together at night. We went possum hunting and coon hunting, and dated girls. One Halloween night we pushed a grouchy old neighbor's pickup truck away from where he parked it near a window; we took off all four of the wheels; and let the frame flat down on the ground. We then, each of us, made a bowel movement and decorated it with lug bolts. My two accomplices did not go to high school.

My Greenway High School friends were mainly basketball players. We had no gymnasium. We played on the bare ground with the dirt court marked with lime. We practiced and played in all kinds of weather.

We played one team that had a gym, which was a real treat. We played in the snow and on frozen ground, but when the ground began to thaw and get muddy, we had to quit. It's hard to dribble the basketball on mud. Even Michael Jordan would have had trouble with that!

Starting in the fall of 1937, I was a sophomore in Greenway High School. Only about one and a half miles, as the crow flies, from our house, I'd cut across fields and follow the creek and it would take about 25 to 30 minutes to walk. A couple of other country boys, Shag Cox and Fuzz Fox, and I, and a couple of Greenway boys comprised the basketball team. The principal of our high school, Mrs. Kennedy, was our coach one year. She didn't pretend to know anything about coaching but we had a pretty good team. Shag was a good shooter and Fuzz and I could run and jump with the best. We never studied.

On bad weather nights, one of the city boys would invite us to spend the night, but if they failed to do so, we'd sneak back into the school house after dark and keep the stove burning and sleep on tables and chairs. We got caught one time and were suspended briefly from school. We played pool after school and after basketball practice.

I don't have any memory of doing much work on the farm during high school. I worked at Stallings' Grocery Store in Piggott on Saturdays and holidays and I guess that is where I got my spending money. We spent a lot of time in the old fashioned farmers' store in Greenway. They kept their bulk candy in a glass case with a sliding door and sometimes we'd slip behind the counter and grab a handful of candy. The owners knew we were doing it but we kept them and their checker-playing, tobacco-chewing customers entertained with our antics. Fuzz and I were known as comedians. One time Fuzz played a trick on me by sticking some mouse turds in the "nigger-toes" (chocolate cream balls) before he gave them to me. After I ate them he told me about it, and to get back at Fuzz, I took his new suede jacket and turned one sleeve inside out and sopped the silk lining in crap at the outside toilet. We were estranged for awhile after that. I've forgotten all the details, but out of that incident Fuzz gave me the nickname of "Giz," and that moniker stuck with me through high school.

I must have helped with the chores and farm work some but what I remember most is working at the grocery store. I'd miss school on certain days and work in the store. I drove dad's car to school sometimes and on dates. One time I was paying more attention to my date than to my driving and I ran off the highway and down into the grassy ditch, but did not turn over. Some grass got caught between the tire and the rim and when dad saw that, I was grounded for quite awhile.

Chapter 16:
Post High School

Sometime during my senior year, I got interested in going to business college and was awarded a $300 scholarship from Draughon's Business College in Memphis. Mom and dad drove me to Hayti, Missouri, to catch the train to Memphis. I remember that mom cried all the way to Hayti, and it was a pretty scary time. I hopped tables as waiter at a boarding house near the medical school on Union Avenue in Memphis. The boarders were medical students. The cooks and housekeepers were black women. That is the first time I had ever been around blacks. We served breakfast and supper to boarders, and it was there that I saw my first grits. The cooks were really characters. I had to walk about ten blocks to business college. I took shorthand, typing and bookkeeping. I started in September 1940. My first visit home was Thanksgiving and I caught a ride with a Pollard boy. He had a Harley Davidson motorcycle and it rained on us all the way, but it sure was nice to be home again.

By the summer of 1941 I could take shorthand and transcribe it fast enough to get a certificate and a job as a bookkeeper at Swift and Company in Memphis. About September 1941, I was transferred to Lake Charles, Louisiana, where I worked as a bookkeeper and file clerk for Swift and Company. I stayed at a boarding house where the Marine Corps recruiting sergeant lived. Also at the boarding house was a feller who was reputed to be a boozer. He frequently asked me to go to the bar with him and one night I did so. We sat on bar stools at the bar, and the bartender set a jigger in front of each of us and filled it with booze and left the bottle sitting on the bar. My buddy started talking to the man on his other side, the bartender was busy with other customers, so, when I finished my jigger, I poured another, then another and maybe another. I was feeling sort of dizzy and I asked the bartender how much I owed and he said 15 cents. I paid him and managed to find my way to the boarding house. I later learned that it was 15 cents per jigger and the bartender didn't know how many jiggers I had drunk.

When Pearl Harbor was bombed on December 7, 1941, I was attending First Baptist Church in Lake Charles. I had no idea where Pearl Harbor was but the news spread and when church let out, there was much excitement. The recruiter signed me up for four years in the United States Marine Corps and I gave my boss two weeks' notice. I remember that my boss pointed out to me that it was not a very smart move because I was making $19.00 per week at Swift and Company and would make only $21.00 per month as a private in the Marine Corps. He said, "Son, if I had known you were not any smarter than that, I wouldn't have hired you in the first place." As it turned out, my four years in the Marine Corps yielded enough G.I. Bill time to put me through college and law school, so maybe it wasn't such a dumb move after all.

Chapter 17:
Semper Fi and Boot Camp

I rode a bus home from Lake Charles and stayed a few days. Dad drove me to Jonesboro where I caught a troop train to San Diego on January 15, 1942. I don't know where the train originated but, for some reason, I was put in charge of the Marines on the train, about 15 or 20 men. The trip to San Diego took three or four days and we stopped along the way, but no more Marines got on board nor were we allowed to get off the train. I don't remember where or how we ate. We rode coach chairs. When the train stopped, we'd lower the windows and lean out and people would give us candy and cigarettes. The train and the barracks were racially segregated. I was singled out for special yelling because our orders showed that I was in charge. We were all scared to death. When we got to the station in San Diego, some mean corporal herded us into a tarp-covered Marine truck. I know we were in civvies but I can't remember what happened to them when we got our government issue. When the truck got to boot camp, someone lowered the end gate and yelled for us to unload. We piled out harum-scarum with Marines screaming obscenities at us, calling us the worse looking bunch of slobs that had ever arrived. It must have been about daylight when we got there.

In January it was a lot warmer in San Diego than in Arkansas, so we were sweating from heat and fright. They asked who was in charge. I told them I was and he jumped in front of me, got hold of my clothing, pulled me up into his face, and yelled, "Shithead, when you address me, call me 'sir'." That first day was the most miserable day of my life. Hurry from one line to another for shots, vaccinations, physical examination (drop your shorts, bend over and grab your ankles, skin your penis back - one insult after another - "Skin it back all the way, you dumbass, unless you are afraid a sheep turd will fall out"). To receive my shots I placed my hand on my hip thinking that would make it handy, and he slapped my hand off my hip and screamed into my face, "Who the fuck do you think you are, Mae West?" They issued underwear, socks, shoes, shirts and pants (both khaki and greens), ill-fitting, and threw them at you as you filed by the quartermaster, always threatening us if we lost anything, especially our dog tags or rifle. I still have nightmares about losing my rifle. We were issued a bayonet and scabbard, ammunition belt and metal mess gear. I had never been to a dentist so I had six cavities and they filled all of them that first day without any pain medicine. It was horrible. They shaved our heads, in case we had head lice, and we were indeed a sorry looking bunch of assholes. We had to do double time (run) from one place to the next. We were finally herded into tents, eight folding canvas cots to the tent, level dirt floor. Each bunk had a sea bag to keep our clothes in. They gave us five minutes to make up our bunks and then fall out to march on the run to chow, throw food into our tin mess gear, sit on benches and eat off wooden tables, allowing us only five minutes to eat. We were ordered to run back to the tent and get dressed in fatigue uniforms for exercise in the dark. There was constant yelling of insults. One light bulb hung down from the center of each tent. We slept in our underwear, lights out, no talking to each other. We were pooped and thoroughly intimidated and they made sure they broke our wills that first day.

Up before daylight the next day, "drop your cocks and grab your socks and hit the deck," get dressed, line up outside the tent for inspection and vigorous exercise, run to chow, everything on the double. If there was a wrinkle in your bed cover, the sergeant ripped it off and yelled at you while you remade your cot. Then you would have to do extra exercises. If one man in your tent messed up, the whole bunch had to use their toothbrushes and wash down the slatted boardwalk leading past the tent. We had one boy from Kentucky who always messed up and we wore out our toothbrushes. Then close-order drill on parade ground, spit and polish our belts and shoes, break down, clean and reassemble our rifles quickly. During close-order drill we were told to count cadence - one misstep and you had to step out in front of the platoon for extra humiliation.

After two or three months of that, we rode a truck to San Luis Obispo for rifle range and double time from the tent to the mountains where targets were located, then back to San Diego boot camp. Boot camp finally finished and we were assigned to units and trucked to Camp Elliott where we had metal double-tiered bunk beds in wooden barracks. We did not have to salute non-commissioned officers anymore, only commissioned officers. We got good food and a much easier life. Boot camp was designed to make us so miserable that we looked forward to getting killed, fighting the Japs.

Camp Elliott was about 15 miles from San Diego and the life style there was luxurious, compared to boot camp, especially the chow. We did not have to march to the chow hall, we could go on our own and we had compartmentalized aluminum plates and wholesome meals, cold delicious milk (my mouth is watering even as I dictate this). Breakfast consisted of creamed beef on toast (called shit on a shingle or SOS), sweet cornbread with beans and meat, or bacon and eggs.

My job at Camp Elliot was company clerk. It appears that Draughon's Business College had cast my Marine Corps duty. I could type, compose letters for the company commander, and correct his grammar and spelling. It was very good duty. I filled out morning reports and payroll records and handed out the mail. Headquarters people were treated better than field people. I prepared passes for leave and furloughs and, in effect, I was the conduit through which orders of the company commander were channeled; therefore, all the men in our company tried to ingratiate themselves with me. They thought I had more influence with the captain than I really did, but I enjoyed the prestige. They teased me about being his pet. At night after the lights were out in the barracks, someone would yell, "What's the color of shit?" and everyone would chorus, "Brown." Then someone would yell out, "I'm white all over except my asshole. What color is it?" and everyone would yell out, "Brown."

Shortly after boot camp, I went on a two-week furlough. I can't remember whether I hitchhiked home or rode a train. It was easy for service people to catch rides during the war. I remember that when I got home we had electric lights and dad had purchased a tractor. I looked sharp in my Marine Corps uniform with my high crown barracks cap. The folks pampered me, no chores expected and I received a hero's welcome. PX cigarettes were cheap and dad loved tailor-mades rather than roll his own with CBC cigarette paper and Country Gentlemen tobacco. I gave cigarettes to all my relatives.

Before my furlough, I was getting liberty about every night and would ride a bus to San Diego and go to bars and dance halls looking for girls. I took dance lessons from a divorced girl and fell in love with her and brought her picture home with me on my furlough. She was beautiful and mom wanted me to marry her and have a baby and maybe I would not be shipped overseas.

I'd take a bus to San Diego every night and go to dance halls where the beautiful girls were plentiful and they swarmed to San Diego from all parts of the country. One of my buddies was company bugler, and both of us, in headquarters company, were pets of the first sergeant, and got liberty passes about every night. When the bugler got drunk, he got mean, both with me and our girlfriends and anyone else in the bar. I always had a hard time getting him on the last bus to Elliott. One night another Marine and I were dragging and carrying him toward the bus stop with one of his arms on each of our shoulders. He jerked his arm loose from me and, with his free fist, he hit the other guy in the face and knocked him down. The bugler leaped over a hedge and escaped while I tried to help the poor guy he knocked down. The bugler was never heard from again.

After two or three months of easy living in Camp Elliott, I was transferred to the 22nd Regiment, sent to Camp Pendleton to live in tents again, getting ready to ship overseas. We had combat training for a few weeks, pretty rugged duty, but not as hostile and demeaning as boot camp. Even though I was still company clerk, I had to train in the field.

Chapter 18:
South Pacific is Terrific

It must have been July or August of 1942 when we boarded the SS Lurline, a luxury liner converted to a troop ship, with 5,000 Marines aboard. I stayed seasick and my friends brought me oranges and crackers from the mess hall. Before you cross the equator the first time, you are a pollywog; afterward, a shellback. There was some sort of ceremony but I was too sick to participate. It took about 30 days to reach the island of Upolu, British Samoa. We had no idea where we would land. We had general quarters two or three times. Sirens sound on the ship warning troops that a submarine is firing at us. Everyone manned a battle station, which kept us scared to death, and we never knew whether it was real or fake for training purposes. We had practiced going down the side of the ship with our rifles and bayonets and backpacks, into Higgins boats. When we saw Samoa, we didn't know if the Japs would shoot at us as we left the Higgins boat and ran ashore. No shots were fired and we set up camp and started digging trenches in the rocky hillsides, expecting that Upolu would be the next island that the Japs would hit. We used picks and shovels and all of us raised blisters on our hands. We set up a kitchen, dug latrines, and set up sickbay manned by a Navy doctor and corpsmen. I was still company clerk and prepared all records for our outfit, payroll, and set up allotments for sending money home for the troops.

The Japs never hit, so after eight months in Upolu, we shipped to Pago Pago, American Samoa. On both islands there were natives who lived in falles, a structure with a wooden floor and a roof made of coconut tree limbs. Some of the troops learned to speak the language and made out with the girls, gave them cigarettes and food for their families. On one of the islands I got appendicitis and a navy doctor operated on me and gave me a circumcision at the same time.

After six months on Pago Pago, I got into the Navy V-12 program, which was supposed to send promising enlisted men to college and then to Officer's Training School, upon completion of which I would be a commissioned officer. I received the Piggott weekly newspaper in the mail and unbeknownst to me, our Company Commander had been reading it. There were articles about the Clay County Judge who had served time for embezzling county funds, and was again a candidate for judge when he got out of prison. There was a lawsuit questioning his eligibility. The Company Commander was one of the officers who interviewed candidates for the V-12 program and one of the questions he asked me was whether I thought the judge would win the election and if so, should he be allowed to serve.

Several of us were shipped back to California where we were supposed to be assigned to a college. Instead, we were summarily transferred to other units, without explanation. I figured that the reason we got kicked out of the V-12 program was that upon closer scrutiny, they decided we were not officer material after all. In 1994, while attending a hospital seminar in California, I happened to meet a nurse who is the daughter of Jack Galvin with whom I went through boot camp, and went to Samoa and who also was booted from the V-12 program. He had learned that the reason we were booted out was that the Corps had lost our records. It was probably lucky for us, because the casualties were very high for Second Lieutenants after they completed Officer Training School.

I was transferred to Military Police Unit, still as company clerk. We had gas coupons and cigarettes and liberty every weekend. We'd hitchhike to L.A. where there were plenty of girls. Usually we'd get them to take us home Sunday night and give them gas coupons and cigarettes. Sometimes they'd drive to Pendleton on Friday afternoon to pick us up and take us to L.A.

One day I saw this pretty black-headed little woman Marine standing outside the PX, holding a black kitten in her arms. I walked up to her and extended my hand toward the kitty and looked her in the eye and said, "May I stroke your pussy?" Those were the first words I every uttered to my wife, Lottie. We started seeing each other, going to movies, so forth, but I continued my weekend trips to L.A. She worked in personnel and found my records and saw that I was born in "UNK" Arkansas. She later learned that stood for "Unknown." One night when I walked her to her barracks, she dared me to come inside. I did so. A guard saw us and it took some fast talking by her to keep him from taking me to the brig. I was a sergeant then and would have certainly been busted to corporal if he had taken me in. Another close call was one Saturday afternoon when, for some reason I did not go to L.A. Another sergeant and I called the camp phone operator on the phone and sang to her, "Going Home on a 499", which was a pregnancy discharge and a dirty word. The operator traced the call, and pretty soon we heard a knock on the door. We were in the company office and had the keys, but we could hear the MPs' voices and heard them refer to a master key, heard keys rattling, and heard them trying different keys in the lock. We were huddled against the wall on the bottom bunk of the company commander's bunk and were very relieved when they gave up.

Probably the reason I did not go to L.A. that weekend was that Lottie and I were getting pretty serious and talking about getting married. I can't remember the details of getting the license, but we went to a justice of the peace in Oceanside on May 31, 1945, and he hitched us. Whoever stood up with us during the wedding ceremony had a car, and we all went to a drive-in and had chicken-in-a-basket and french fries. We spent that afternoon on the beach at Laguna Beach. We rented a trailer in a trailer park and, I believe, I had already received my shipping orders to go overseas. We had enough money to rent for one week and I wrote or wired home for dad to send me the $200 I had sent home by allotment from Samoa. I asked him to wire it to me but there was a mix up and it did not arrive timely. I wrote dad a bitter, hateful letter only to learn later that Western Union was to blame. I have regretted many times writing that awful letter. I think I shipped out a few days later. We did not buy a diaphragm or orthogynal gel until two or three days after the wedding so Lottie was pregnant and went home on a 499 discharge about October 1945. I was in Guam. Lottie's sister, Freda, and Abe got married two or three days before we did, unannounced. Lottie got a letter from her sister telling her to sit down before reading the letter because it would be so shocking that the news might knock her down, having no idea that Lottie was even considering marriage. Freda was a nurse in the Navy and was sent to Okinawa and came to Guam to see me.

When I learned that Lottie was pregnant, I wrote three long letters from Guam telling her why I wanted the kid to be raised non-Jewish. One point I made was that Jews were discriminated against in so many ways that I felt we owed it to the kid not to burden him or her with known pitfalls. There were no Jews in the neighborhoods where I had grown up, and I don't think I was really aware that Jews were of a different religion or anything of that nature, but I must have experienced something along the way to make me think that Jews had a hard time or at least were the brunt of some discrimination.

VJ Day was in July or August 1945. Our company was involved with patrolling a certain area of Guam, and Jap snipers would pick them off regularly. As company clerk I did not have to patrol by jeep but the corporal, who replaced me after I was sent to the holding pool to await transportation back to the States, got bored sitting in the office and he went out on jeep patrol and was killed before I left Guam. We were guarding supplies, ammunition, small arms, etc. and we would use our rifle butts to break open crates so we could steal the contents. At 5:00 p.m. we had beer call. Warm beer really spewed when we opened the cans. If you were looking toward the sun in late afternoon, the spewing beer looked like a rainbow. The Pacific is beautiful on the corals of Guam. I got such a tan that I looked like a gook (native), resulting in several skin cancers in recent years. The heavy military action in Guam took place before I arrived and most of the coconut trees had been damaged by bombs and artillery units. We lived in tents in Guam. We boarded ship, bound for the USA, in December 1945. You got to go home according to a point system. My four-year enlistment was expiring on January 14, 1946, and the point system and my expiration date happened to coincide.

Chapter 19:
Back to My Civvies - Post-War Problems

My mustering out pay was a couple of hundred dollars and I think they paid for my train ticket, maybe only per mile to Arkansas where I joined. I think I rode a train from San Diego to New York City where big-bellied Lottie met me at Penn Station.

When she first got to Hoboken, pregnant, I don't think she had told her parents (the last thing her father had said to her as she left home to go to the Marine Corps, was, "Don't disgrace us."). She had to tell them about the marriage as her tummy got too big to hide. She had to live with them for a while, and then found a basement two-room apartment, no refrigerator. We kept our perishables in an orange crate outside our window. She told her parents my name was Brownstein. They spoke Yiddish and only broken English, both of them foreign born. They bought us a bed and a baby crib, and Lottie's Uncle Ben gave us a used refrigerator sometime after Ron was born. We were flat broke and my mustering out pay wouldn't last long, so I started looking for a job the next day after I got to Hoboken. I worked as a clerk typist and bookkeeper at National City Bank of New York on Wall Street. I walked from our apartment to Barclay Street Ferry, paid ten cents, took my lunch in a paper bag, and walked twelve blocks from where the ferry landed, to Wall Street. One time I mistakenly threw my lunch away instead of the garbage and at lunch time when I opened my paper sack, I was very disappointed. I had grown up and lived all my life in the boondocks, so downtown Manhattan, New York City was fascinating to me. I would have worked for free if we had had something to live on. The Horn and Hardart Automat, and Neddick street-side orange juice stands, and men selling hotdogs out of push carts were all very interesting.

I made a small salary and soon noticed that the college boys would visit our department for a couple of weeks, then go to another department. My boss told me that they were making more money than he did after 35 years working at the bank, without a college degree. That got me to thinking and, meanwhile, Lottie was getting bigger and bigger and her Bubby (Yiddish for grandma) predicted a mid-February arrival. We had picked out a name for a girl, after Bubby. Lottie wanted me to go to college, and she started typing letters to colleges, mainly to the East Coast colleges.

One night after Hymie, Lottie's brother, got discharged from the Army, we invited him to our apartment for dinner. Lottie had heard me talk about mom's fried chicken and gravy so she started frying the chicken while Hymie and I visited. We talked and we talked, and the chicken fried and fried and fried, and the vegetables she was cooking got overdone. We finally discovered that what she was frying was a roasting hen; she didn't realize there was a difference between a frying chicken and a roasting hen.

On the night that Ronnie arrived, Lottie had invited her Marine Corps friend and another girl who lived on Long Island for dinner but, before they arrived, labor pains began and Hymie took Lottie to Margaret Hague Hospital in Jersey City. I took Lottie's friends out to eat. I did not go to the hospital that night but during the night I learned that it was a boy, and the next morning Hymie took me to the hospital. I got very upset when it appeared that Lottie was consulting Hymie, rather than me, about whether to have Ronnie circumcised by the doctor or by a Rabbi.

I think the taxpayers paid the doctor and hospital bill for Ronnie's birth. Those were very tense times. I drew $20.00 per week for 52 weeks from the government and I believe Lottie did too. The war effort had depleted civilian clothing and, somehow, I had emerged from the Marine Corps with the suit I wore on the train going to boot camp. I don't remember where my civilian suit was while I was in the Marine Corps, but I do remember I wore it to work at the bank. Where that double-breasted brown tweed suit was during the four years I was in the Marines is still a mystery. It was probably at the bottom of my sea bag for four years.

In March or April 1946, we worked more frantically on college. When the weather got warm my winter suit was too heavy to wear to work so I wore Marine Corps khaki. One night in our hot apartment I was nude, drying the dishes, and Lottie's Aunt Jenny descended the steps into our basement apartment. Our window was raised and she lifted the shade to announce her arrival and saw me in the nude and she staggered inside and fell into a chair saying, "I didn't see notting" (broken English). If Lottie would only chronicle her childhood. It was ten times more interesting than mine. Her relatives were characters and she has many funny, funny stories.

Ron was born on February 26, 1946. We brought him home from the hospital about March 3rd. Ida (Lottie's mother) bought us a crib and our bedroom suite and that filled one of our rooms. Lottie's friends were mostly Italian and Spanish. Shortly after we brought Ron home, the weather was cold, and one of Lottie's Spanish friends and her mother, Mrs. Pablos, came to see us. Mrs. Pablos walked straight to the crib, picked up Ron with her cold hands and kissed him on or near the lips, all while speaking Spanish, which I could not understand. I tried to tell her not to awaken him. The daughter said her mom just wanted to hug him, and I yelled, "Hug him, my balls!" It scared them so badly that they left, leaving nice baby gifts behind.

I continued riding the ferry to work and we kept talking about college. Bubby bought us a baby buggy and, with mosquito netting over the baby carriage, she pushed Ron to the 10th Street Park, found a bench in a sunny spot with the sun shining on him, and sat and rocked him gently for hours on end. Wholesome food, fresh air and sunshine were her recipe for good health. She could not even speak broken English. She and I could not communicate at all, but she was such a sweet old lady that I learned to love her. She and Lottie spoke Yiddish and Lottie was her favorite grandchild. I think we have Bubby on film.

We probably did not let Harry and Ida (I called them pop and mom) know that we were thinking about college. I applied to two colleges on the East Coast and the University of Arkansas. I think Hymie got into Stephens College in Hoboken. I don't remember Freda and Abe being around at that time. When I was accepted at U of A, we told mom and pop, and I gave notice to my boss that I was quitting. Pop had grown up on a farm in Lithuania, and he told Lottie that she would have to milk cows, feed the chickens, etc. None of them had ever seen a cotton patch. Mom was afraid Ron would be scalped by Indians. We sold the bedroom suite and crib for about half of what mom paid for them, and we sold the fridge. Hymie took us to Penn Station and we rode the train to Memphis.

Chapter 20:
The Hoboken Jew on The Farm

Dad had a car but he did not dare drive to Memphis, so he got the sheriff of Clay County to drive him to the train station in Memphis to meet us. Ron was about four or five months old and Lottie was breast feeding him. Ida fixed us sandwiches to eat on the train and we got to Memphis about dark. Lottie thought all farms had windmills and white picket fences leading up a shady lane to a big white house, etc. Fortunately, it was dark when we got to the farm so she could not see how shoddy it looked, but we could smell the new mown hay. Mom had fried some dried apple pies which we ate with cold milk. I remember mom asking Lottie if she was "full-blooded Jew." Lottie said, "yes," and stuck out her arm and said, "See, my skin looks just like yours."

We had an electric refrigerator and running water in the faucets in the kitchen, but no bathroom. Lottie was horrified to use the outdoor toilet with the Sears and Roebuck catalog as toilet paper. The way our privy was built, as soon as the crap hit the ground, the chickens would eat it.

That summer was a nightmare for Lottie. She tried to raise Ron by Doctor Spock's book. Farm women haul out their tits and nurse their babies publicly, but Lottie always found a way to hide to nurse Ron. My folks thought that was silly. We had to build a fire under a big iron kettle, draw well water, boil the water with lye soap in it, then boil dirty diapers and wrench (rinse) them in a dish pan of clean water and hang them on the clothes line. Ron got diarrhea (mom called it summer complaint), and Lottie wanted Ron to be seen by a doctor, but Mom said that all he needed was a bottle of iced tea. In those days, the doctors made house calls and I don't remember how we got word to the doctor in Piggott to come out, but he did. After he examined Ron, he prescribed iced tea. Of course, mom and Reba made much of that. Lottie felt that dad and Don liked her and were sympathetic and supportive and nice to her during that difficult time, but that mom and Reba not so. I was not as supportive of Lottie as I should have been and I'd have to say that mom was more hateful toward Lottie than I expected. In fact, I did not think my sainted mother was capable of a mean streak.

Somehow we made it through the summer. Lottie did not attend church and I probably didn't either, but we would all go to visit relatives on Sunday afternoons. I remember one Sunday we were sitting on Uncle Raymond and Aunt Edna's front porch after dinner. The hog pasture was directly across the road from the porch and Lottie observed that one of the sows looked pregnant, and that plagued (embarrassed) Aunt Edna because women did not use that word in mixed company. Lottie was always pulling a faux pas like that. Lottie was fascinated by mom's cooking (no recipes). Lottie tried to learn how to milk cows but her crippled finger got in the way. She did manage to pick 36 pounds of cotton one day. The rest of us could pick two or three hundred pounds per day. Lottie heard dad talking about "pushing" the hogs to get them fat enough to slaughter. "Pushing" meant to ply them with food but Lottie was picturing him behind the hog literally pushing it around the hog lot. The whole farm vocabulary was strange to her. When we referred to the rooster's or the hen's comb, she pictured a hair comb.

Lottie loved the farm food, mom's biscuits, fried chicken and gravy, fresh garden vegetables, etc. The cream separator fascinated her. She still remembers mom making fresh butter by shaking a one-half gallon mason jar full of cream. After mom mashed up a big pot of potatoes, she put the pot under the cream spout and mixed rich, fresh cream in to the mashed potatoes. Lottie couldn't believe her eyes when she saw dad cut a big slab of butter off the butter ball, pour sorghum molasses on it, mix it up and ladle that mixture onto a hot biscuit. That was breakfast dessert, after he had eaten biscuits and gravy and fried potatoes and fried sow belly and fried chicken, in season.

Chapter 21:
Look Out College. Here I Come.

I made about $10 per day picking cotton for about four weeks before we left for University of Arkansas in Fayetteville. School was supposed to start on September 10th. Dad drove us to Hoxie where we caught a train. There was a long layover in Little Rock and we arrived in Fayetteville late at night. I don't remember where we spent the night but we learned the next day that, because of the influx of veterans coming to college on the G.I. Bill, the housing project where we were supposed to live would not be ready until October 15th. We got on the train and went back to Piggott and I picked cotton. Mom made Ron's aprons (dresses) out of flour sacks. I think he was crawling and beginning to walk. Lottie hated for him to crawl around on the floor where we walked with our cow manure shoes.

Dad bought us a Stromberg-Carlson radio for $30.00 and that was our source of entertainment, besides Ron who was developing into a happy little boy, wearing flour sack aprons and always needing a haircut - but always laughing.

When we got to Fayetteville on October 15th, school did start but Terry Village was still not quite ready for occupancy so we found us an apartment in an old house. We cooked on a hot plate. The toilet was in the basement and it would not flush. I had to carry a pail of water from the kitchen sink to flush it. Big rats were plentiful in the basement, and I had to sit with Lottie and hold her hand when she used the pot. We had a playpen for Ron and I was nervous about my studies and would get upset when Ron cried at night and I would spank him because that was the way I was raised. Lottie knew better, but I'm afraid I was a mean dad.

I think we lived in the apartment until January or February 1947. We had a wood burning heating stove. I remember Lottie and I were stacking the fire wood and Ron was watching us through the window, wearing an apron, jumping up and down, snotty-nosed, laughing all the time, and always needing a haircut. When we started feeding him food to supplement the breast milk, I'd rattle pots and pans to distract him while Lottie shoveled food into his mouth. The fire wood would burn out during the night, the room would be cold when we woke up, and Ron would be standing there with his wet diaper and wet pajamas, snotty-nosed, long-hair, waiting for us to wake up. I'd stick him in the bed with Lottie, I'd rekindle the fire, then jump back under the cover until the room got warm. He'd crawl all over us. We had no car but we lived close enough to the grocery store that Lottie walked and pushed the baby buggy to get the groceries. Our only income was the G.I. allowance, either $75 or $95 per month. We skimped every way we could. I studied all the time and Lottie took care of Ronnie. I think every military person received $20 per week for 52 weeks to help them get by until they could re-enter civilian life and find a job. Maybe our 52-20 check didn't come until January or February of 1947. I took up tickets at football games and earned a little that way. Also, I got ten cents per interview working for a survey company. When I took my first test, I made good grades and then felt confident that I would be able to handle college work. As a matter of fact, I made all A's the first year and was elected to Phi Beta Kappa Fraternity.

When Terry Village was ready, we were thrilled. Pure luxury. They were barracks that had been moved to Fayetteville from Fort Chaffee, but they were new and clean. One bedroom, living room, and small kitchen table with stove and refrigerator, $30 per month, including utilities, less than we had been paying for the dump. We even had a gas furnace. It was about a quarter mile from campus, steep uphill going, and downhill coming home. Probably in 1947 or 1948 we decided that Lottie should go to college and take enough courses to qualify for the G.I. Bill. Our allotment went from $95.00 a month to $105 per month. She just chose subjects that did not conflict with mine. There was a ten-minute break between classes. My class would be over at ten minutes before the hour and I would meet her halfway down the hill as she was rushing to class. We trained Ron not to move from the chair until we got home. One time one of the neighbors came over during the break, but Ron would not move out of the chair until I got home.

A professor lived near us and Lottie used to babysit for them and snitch a few cigarettes and eat from their fridge. Their little girl and Ron became fast friends. At the end of each semester a few of the Terry Village residents would graduate and move out and many of them would leave or give away some of their furniture, and we picked up a few items like that. Somebody gave us some kitchen curtains with big red strawberries on them, but we hung them in the living room where we needed them worse, to replace the bed sheets we had been using. Lottie washed the diapers on a rub board until we inherited a portable washing machine from some graduate, another luxury.

We were sailing along fine until we learned that Lottie was pregnant again with Cliff in the summer of 1948. She had to quit school, which decreased our allowance, but we knew the ropes better and were picking up odd jobs. Lottie worked at a concession stand at the movie house.

I took a series of aptitude tests which pointed me toward law school. I did not know any lawyer, and had no idea what they did, but it sounded important. I ascertained that my G.I. Bill would last long enough to get a law degree. I got my B.A. degree in 1948 and started to law school. Cliff arrived in February 1949, and we got a two bedroom apartment, and rent went up to $35.00 per month. I had let up a little on my studies before law school and made a few B's and one C. I buckled down again when I started law school. I went to the Law Library every night after we got the boys to bed.

When I was in law school, the first Afro-American was admitted. The South was still segregated then and in order to avoid trouble with red necks, the dean had a door removed from a closet and put two boards across the door and the black student was thus segregated from the rest of us. That arrangement continued until the dean learned that a reporter - photographer from Life magazine - was coming to the law school, so we integrated overnight.

Jobs were scarce in the summer and fall of 1950. Since I had gone to summer school every year, I was finishing at midterm in January

1951. The only job interview I had was with Maurice Cathey from Paragould. He had made arrangements through the law school to set up interviews with the three top students. That must have been in October or November of 1950. I can't remember much about the interview. I must have been the third one he interviewed because he wanted to meet Lottie. He drove me to Terry Village. Lottie was washing diapers and baking a pie. She was rolling dough and had flour all over her face and hair. She hurriedly dressed while I found a neighbor to babysit for us. When she saw Mrs. Cathey's full length mink coat, she had visions of sugar plums floating around in her head. We went to Hynie's Steakhouse on the Springdale Highway, one of the best in Northwest Arkansas at that time. I was too nervous to enjoy my steak, but shortly thereafter, I was hired as an associate in the Kirsch and Cathey Law Firm, starting in February of 1951, at the princely salary of $200.00 per month, which sounded enormous to us. Mr Cathey gave me two or three things to research after the interview and that's about all I did the rest of the school year - write memoranda of law for him. I had made good enough grades to get excused from final exams.

Chapter 22:
I'm a Lawyer Now. Show Me a Courtroom

At Christmas of 1950 we rode the train to Piggott and I used my father's pickup truck to drive from Piggott to Paragould every day, except Christmas Day, and worked like a trojan for two whole weeks. I think we took a train back to Fayetteville after Christmas.

We remembered how hard it was to buy things during World War II so when the Korean Conflict was starting, we tried to buy a washing machine in Fayetteville but none was available. One of our friends who had a car drove us to Fort Smith and we bought a washing machine with a suds saver and a dryer and had them shipped to Paragould. We had accumulated quit a bit of furniture from the graduating students over the years.

In early February 1951, I went back to Piggott and borrowed dad's pickup truck to move us to Paragould. Mr. Cathey had found us an apartment - really we occupied the ground floor of a barny old house. We loaded our junk on the pickup, and looked like "Grapes of Wrath." We couldn't bring ourselves to throw anything away because we were so insecure. I remember that the last thing I loaded was an old lawn chair. The canvas was worn out and it stuck out from under the tarp. We stopped at the dairy where we owed a balance on the milk bill as we left Fayetteville. We had a flat between Newport and Hoxie. The jack and the spare tire were covered with all our junk but we managed to get it fixed.

The old house where we were going to live had stained-glass windows, and a coal stove for heat. The couple who lived upstairs drank salty dogs every Saturday night. He was a trucker and was gone all week. She dipped snuff and the stairway from their apartment led into our kitchen. She'd come down and visit, walk to the stove and raise the lid and spit her snuff juice into the fire. About every Saturday night they would get drunk. One Saturday night they got drunk and she came running down the stairs, had a double-barrel shotgun in one hand and two shells in the other, and her wire-rim glasses were bent, hanging on one ear. She wanted me to load the gun so she could shoot the son-of-a-bitch upstairs. Of course, I refused, but as we told the story later, it always came out that Lottie wanted me to oblige her, thus creating an opportunity to get my first criminal case!

There was a two-week term of Circuit Court starting in Paragould On March 7, 1951, and I was going to try a jury case. I was so nervous that on Saturday before my trial on Monday, I developed seven boils under my right arm and the doctor shot penicillin into the head of each boil. I must have been allergic to penicillin because I broke out in a rash, especially the bottom of my feet and the palms of my hands. I got through the trial, almost a cinch to win. My farmer client was having his load of grain weighed on the gin scales when the scales broke, fell and damaged his truck. The jury returned a verdict in our favor for $500.00. Big deal!

I was given shitty jobs, filling out 1040s, running errands, doing research and running down witnesses. I had a portable Underwood typewriter and would type out a witness's statement, with the portable sitting on my lap, and get the witness to sign it. State Farm Insurance Company had no adjuster in Northeast Arkansas, so I investigated car wrecks all over Northeast Arkansas. The statements which I took from witnesses were mailed to the insurance company by Mr. Cathey who would make recommendation whether to pay or deny the claim. If the latter, and suit was filed, Mr. Cathey would handle the court case. Mr. Kirsch and Mr. Cathey would try to get clients to let me handle their legal work, but most wanted one of them. I had an extension phone on my desk and I would listen to their phone calls. One day Mr. Kirsch was trying to get his client to let me handle it and the client said, "Goddam it, Will, I'm sure that new kid is bright, but this ain't no fuckin' sharecroppin' case, you know. I know the boy has to learn on somebody, but not me."

Cliff was two and Ron was five when we moved to Paragould. I worked six and a half days and seven nights a week. I had no car and walked to the office. When I hunted witnesses, I used Mr. Kirsch's car. I recited poetry to the boys. Ron could already recite some of them and Cliff was trying, even at age two. About June 1951 we found a small rent house. The owner had a nervous breakdown, and was confined in an institution. Her brother told us we could rent it for at least a year. It was partially furnished but we moved our washer and dryer. Cliff and Ron slept on bunk beds, Ron upper, Cliff lower. No more flour sack dresses in Paragould. When I'd come home to eat supper, Lottie was whipped, trying to corral two boys, cook, clean house, etc. I'd take care of the boys. When they heard the door opening, they'd come running and both of them would jump on me and we'd roll and rumble on the floor. I'd skin-the-cat and had to make sure I skinned Cliff as many times as Ron. Both would squeal with delight when they hit the floor. After supper I'd bathe them and put their pajamas on and read them stories, and then go back to the office and work for a couple of hours.

I worked for $300 a month in 1952, $400 a month in 1953 and $500 per month in 1954. In 1955 I was made a partner which means I received a percentage of the firm's income. Many times at night and on weekends, I'd sneak a look at the books and try to identify what my labors were producing. I knew they were screwing me and I'd come home and bitch to Lottie but was too insecure to confront them. When you've got a wife and two kids, living from month-to-month, the prospect of losing your job is indeed daunting!

About 1952 or '53 I lost a trial which Mr. Cathey thought I should have won and he was so critical that he convinced me that I would never be a good trial lawyer. Lottie and I put together a resumé and we mailed it to about 25 big companies. We went to Memphis one Sunday, and Lottie and the boys visited with the man's wife, while he interviewed me for a job selling insurance, at a small salary plus commission. He lived in a nice house in the Overton Park area and looked very prosperous. Lottie and I both knew that I was no salesman - couldn't sell beer on a troop train - so we decided to stay put.

Chapter 23:
A Family Grows in Paragould

After I got a raise or two, Mr. Kirsch sold us his old car when he got a new one, on credit, no papers. He just had the car title put in my name - another reason we couldn't move to Memphis. I guess he knew that that would tie me to the law firm. We did enjoy it, the very first car we ever owned, and we started visiting my folks in Piggott on Sand Creek. They would visit us in Paragould and bring eggs and fresh garden vegetables, canned fruit, and so forth.

Somewhere along the line, mom and dad converted to Church of Christ from Methodist and mom became fanatical in her zeal to convert us. She did not have much hope for Lottie, but hoped the boys and I would see the light. She'd slip religious tracts into my pockets and briefcase. She was convinced she would spend eternity in hell because she did not "see the light" early enough to save her kids. My brother, Don, married a Utah Mormon and mom went through the same thing with them. World War II really caused an uprooting and upheaval of population - New Jersey, Utah and Arkansas.

About 1953 we had to give up the rent house, but found another one about two blocks further from the office. It was bigger, had less traffic on the street which diminished Lottie's worries about the boys playing outside. They had graduated to bicycles, and had boyfriends next door and across the street. The house was already plumbed for washer and dryer. We had a car and Lottie learned to drive (her parents never owned or drove a car).

After I was made partner in 1955, near year end I was invited to attend the firm meeting, when the division of funds was discussed. I had examined the books in advance and knew how much income I was generating. I raised so much hell about the proposed division; I threatened to leave; and we had to have another meeting. I ended up with about $10,000, and bought a brand new blue and white Ford station wagon for $4,800. Lottie was working part time in the circuit clerk's office. We farmed the boys out to different sitters. I stumped the county for one of our judges who was running for governor, and he won. To the victor go the spoils, and Lottie went to work full time as a payroll clerk in the Highway Department. One of the politicos who was on the winning side in the governor's race kicked the losers out of the Highway Department and put Lottie and others in. He sold us our first TV, a blonde RCA, which the boys dearly loved. Two years later the governor was beaten and Lottie got kicked out of the Highway Department, but I was then a partner and we were in pretty good shape financially. In 1955 our lease expired on the rent house and we found another one on Twelfth Street.

In early 1956 Lottie and I decided to try for a girl. We left the boys with the sitter, left the condoms at home, got into our car and went to Little Rock for a bar association meeting. We stayed at the Grady Manning Hotel. Lottie got pregnant and Bunny arrived in October of '56, the only one we had on purpose. Ron was conceived before we bought the diaphragm and Cliff resulted from a misplaced diaphragm. Diaphragms and condoms delayed Bunny's arrival until we were ready.

While I was in law school we usually found a way for Lottie to visit her family about every year. When Ron was about a year and a half old, Lottie took him on the train to New Jersey. When I was in law school we caught a ride to New Jersey with a professor, and he had the car so full of his own stuff that we stuck Ron on top of his things in the backseat and Lottie and I took turns holding Cliff in our laps. We fed him pabulum and it was always a problem to get the milk warmed for the pabulum because the professor was always in a hurry. We would struggle to get finished eating in a hurry, and he would wait impatiently and let us know that he was ready to go. He was too tight to stop at a motel. I'd pay for the gasoline. He drove us to Rockaway Beach, Long

Island, where Ida was spending the summer. She had a second floor apartment and as soon as we arrived, Lottie's nephew, who was visiting, promptly pushed Cliff down the stairs, causing a concussion. A doctor who lived on the ground floor examined him and advised us what to do. The boys loved the beach, the strong undertow, the big waves, and the cold water. Ida would bring fruit and sandwiches to the beach. There was a boardwalk and play land nearby.

On one of our trips in our station wagon, which had no air conditioning, we drove with the windows down and with an ice chest full of soft drinks and sandwiches, and a pallet in the rear for the boys. Lottie would soak a wash cloth in the ice chest and rub the back of my neck. We stopped near Columbus, Ohio, to get a motel with a pool. One time the boys forgot their swimsuits and I tried to coax them to the unoccupied pool in their underwear, but they were so modest that every time they thought someone was coming to swim, they'd scamper back to the motel.

Riding the waves at Rockaway Beach was great fun. Lottie and the boys were better swimmers than I. I dog-paddled, like all farm boys who learned to swim in a mud hole in the creek. The beach was two or three blocks from Ida's apartment and when we wanted to answer a call of nature, we would go into the ocean. Once when Ron needed to do number two, I coaxed him out into the deep water so that he could lower his swimsuit enough to get the job done. He was mortified when the waves washed the turds back to the beach. On weekends, Lottie's father would ride the train to Rockaway Beach and bring goodies for the kids. He wore a big straw hat and long-sleeved robe. He covered himself from head to toe, never went into the water, and just loved the sand and the wind. He was about five feet tall, wiry, a fast moving house painter, probably the best in Hoboken.

On one of our trips to the East Coast, I took the boys to Shea Stadium to see a baseball game (it might have been Yankee or Dodger Stadium). I went to the concession stand to get us some refreshments. I ordered a "hot dog," and the concessionaire asked if I mean "frankfurter." The Chicago Cubs were playing that evening. The man who was working in the concession stand asked me if I was from "Chicagah." I told him I was from Arkansas, and he said, "Jeese, that's even woise."

About 1955 I filed 1040s for the Balks and my mom and dad and had them pay in a little self-employment tax. Neither of them had ever filed before, and I prepared one every year until they died, the smartest move I ever made. I don't know how they would have gotten by without Social Security and Medicare in later years.

We lived in the rent house on Twelfth Street about a year. We still had the car I had bought from Mr. Kirsch. The house was on a hill and our gravel driveway was quite steep. One day I drove by the house to pick up something I had forgotten to take to work that morning, and I thought I had left the car in gear so it could not roll down the hill. After I closed the door and was about half way between the car and the house, I heard gravel crunching and looked around and saw my pretty blue Ford headed down the hill. I started chasing it so fast that I came out of one of my shoes but managed to catch it, opened the door and get in and get on the brakes just before it crashed into the house at the bottom of the hill.

When Bunny arrived in October of 1956, Ronnie was ten and Cliffy was seven. I don't remember how Lottie got to the hospital. I suppose the boys were in school. I just remember the joy I felt when the nurse told me that it was a girl. I wanted to see for myself. I supposed I worked harder than ever after I went on a percentage and had three kids to feed and clothe.

In the spring of 1957 we bought the house on Highland Street and lived there from 40 years.

When we were taking a trip to New Jersey about 1958 or 1959, when Arkansas and Faubus were getting nationwide bad press regarding the Little Rock Central High School segregation matter, we were traveling on the Pennsylvania Turnpike and a car behind us kept honking and turning its headlights on and off. We thought they were heckling us because of our Arkansas license so we ignored them. They finally pulled alongside our car. They were Afro-Americans and I was afraid to stop. I slowed down and they finally went on and then we heard a flat tire flopping and we realized that is what they were trying to tell us - that we had a flat tire. We went to New Jersey every summer after we got the station wagon.

After we moved to Highland Street we had lots of room. The boys had single beds upstairs (they slept together in a double bed at first). We put Bun's crib in our bedroom downstairs and kept it there until she asked me why I took my clothes off at night and fought with mommy - then the guest room upstairs became Bunny's bedroom.

About that time, Bunny was three or four, my law partner, Maurice Cathey, and his family (including teenage daughter, Ann) lived across the street from us. The kids obviously heard Lottie and me comment on how helpless and spoiled Ann was and probably heard us say that they probably had to wipe her butt after a BM. Mr. Cathey came to visit us, he picked Bunny up, as he talked to her, she asked him, "Who wipes Ann?" I can't remember much about my playing with the boys after Bun came. I know I was still strict with them, made them write themes every summer. I'd correct their spelling and grammar and give them written grades. I spanked and whipped them occasionally. One time I told them to do something in my absence and as the time approached when they knew I'd be coming home, they still had not done the chore. They figured I'd spank them with my belt. They put on so many pants to cushion the blows and looked so bloated, I busted out laughing and hugged them and skipped the whipping altogether.

Chapter 24:
Lawyering

After about five years of dirty work, we hired an associate which allowed me to develop my skills as an advocate, and soon I was doing more trial work and less paperwork. I had so much success with juries in Clay County (my home county), that my reputation spread. Martindale-Hubble, a company which ranks lawyers all over the United States, according to their ability, used me as one of its rating experts in Northeast Arkansas. As I later learned, lawyering is more difficult than judging.

One trial comes to mind wherein I was representing an old farmer, probably 75 years old, who had a new Cadillac which was involved in an accident with an ambulance, attempting to pass him as he was pulling off the highway onto a dirt road leading to his home. He wore bib overalls and used salty country expressions. He testified that the ambulance was speeding and was so far behind him when he started his turn that he had plenty time to clear. Finally, on cross-examination, he admitted that he failed to give a signal (at first he said he thought he did, and then he couldn't remember). Finally, he said, "Okay, let's just let the hide go with the taller" (that is, let the bad go along with the good). We lost the case. When he heard the jury's verdict that it was his fault and that he owed $2,500, he stood up, reached into his hip pocket, took out his billfold, walked around in front of the bench, and asked the judge, "Your Honor, do I pay you the money?"

In another case, one involving child custody, the parties had divorced, and the wife had custody of two little boys. I represented the husband and we took her to court to try to get visitation rights for the husband. We sat in the courtroom all day waiting for our case to be heard. The mother was there with her sons. About 30 minutes before time to adjourn court, my client said he and his wife had agreed upon a settlement, and wanted to talk to the lawyers. They wanted to remarry. I held one child, and the other lawyer held the other child, and we stood with them while the judge performed the wedding ceremony.

One of the funniest courtroom episodes that I can remember happened in the early years of my law practice. An elderly lady was charged with murdering her neighbor. She couldn't afford to hire an attorney, and that was way before we had paid public defenders, so the judge would simply appoint one of the lawyers practicing in that county to defend the indigent defendant. In this case, Judge Charles Light appointed me to defend her because, in following the rotation, it was simply my time to take a charity case. The lady I was defending had stabbed her neighbor with a butcher knife because she thought had poisoned her cat. We didn't have much of a defense, so she was convicted, and Judge Light sentenced her to 25 years in prison. She stood up and said, "Judge, Your Honor, I'm 75 years old, and I may not be able to serve 25 years." Judge Light just looked at her very solemnly and said, "Well, Miss Annie, just do as much as you can and we'll forget about the rest."

When I first started practicing law in 1951, some cases could still be filed in the Justice of the Peace courts. On trial day, either side could demand a jury. The JP would go out and get three guys off the street and they would be the jury. I did that one time in Powhatan Courthouse, which is now a museum and is a registered National Historic Building. I recently paid a $3.00 admission fee to get inside and look around the museum.

About 1962 Maurice Cathey and I built a new building for our law firm. Mr. Kirsch would not participate because he thought carpeted floors were too fine for his clients. We prospered, hired more associates, and I was the lead trial attorney in the firm. We had to split the firm income so many ways that my share would run around $60,000 per year.

Many lawyers refuse to accept divorce cases, especially if there is a child custody question involved. Most divorce cases seemed to grow out of a situation in which the wife thinks that her husband has been cheating on her, and, "Hell hath no fury like the wrath of woman scorned." Many times the irate wife will become convinced that her husband has been sexually abusing their daughter, and will insist that her lawyer air that out in court. Frequently, it is obvious that the little girl has been coaxed by her mother into making that charge and, usually, the little girl is too scared to testify in court. The husband's denial is usually more convincing, and it usually doesn't set well with the judge when there is no evidence to go on, except the half-hearted testimony of the child. It doesn't take much evidence to convince her that her husband is capable of the most heinous of crimes.

I remember one case in which the wife was fighting mad because, in typing the complaint, the husband's lawyer's secretary had mistakenly mistyped "general indignities" so that it read "veneral indignities," and the wife thought he was accusing her of having a venereal disease.

In another case, a woman lived in Leachville, which meant that I had to file the divorce in Blytheville in Mississippi County, 50 miles away. The husband was a substantial farmer, and was not really opposed to the divorce, but was trying to minimize the property settlement and the amount he would have to pay in alimony and support. We litigated hard all day in Blytheville, but didn't quite get finished. I felt that our evidence came out pretty well, and that we stood a good chance to get a substantial settlement, but the wife called me about 5:00 the next morning, woke me up, and told me that she had decided she wanted to "put in for the medicine cabinet." Even though I told her the day before that I thought we had a good chance of winning big money, she was so bitter to get the last drop of blood, she wanted to make a fuss about the medicine cabinet.

One of the funniest cases that I ever presided over when I was Chancery Judge grew out of a divorce in which the husband had brought suit, claiming that his wife had had sexual intercourse with her father-in-law, the husband's own father. The wife admitted to the sexual relations but claimed that she reluctantly did so after the mother-in-law died, and her husband had told her that the father needed sex in order to stay healthy and live longer. The old man had no teeth and was wearing bib overalls and had a very country twang in his voice, with hillbilly expressions. He testified that the first time it happened, he went by his son's house and was going to help him build a hog pen, and the wife said he had gone somewhere to get some musky-dines (muscadines), but should be back any minute. She invited him into the house and disappeared into another room and shortly reappeared wearing nothing but what she was born with, "neked as a jay bird," and said she was taking a bath and wanted him to wash her back. He thought that was strange because he hadn't "heered any water runnin," but she did get into the bath tub and start the water and wanted him to help. When she "reched up and unbuckled my overall gallus, I said, 'uh-oh oldman, you're in trouble'. When she got my britches off, she got out of the tub and led me to her bed and she was so wet, I kept slippin' off of her." The attorney who was questioning the old man got tickled, and we had to recess court for several minutes until we all regained our composure.

In a case in which I represented the husband in a divorce case, my client sat to my left at the counsel table, and the wife's lawyer sat to my right, with his client to his right. We were trying to prove that the wife had a "bottle" problem, which was the cause of their domestic discord. In truth and in fact, the wife's attorney had a severe bottle problem and had the reputation for same. His wife was a school teacher and she would make unannounced visits to his office and search everywhere and find his booze, usually vodka, and pour it into the commode. He developed some very ingenious hiding places for his bottle. When my client was on the stand, the opposing attorney was cross-examining him about his testimony that on one occasion the wife had been intoxicated. The attorney asked him whether he had seen her take a drink, and he admitted that he had not, and he asked him what kind of liquor she drank and be testified vodka. The lawyer then asked him how he knew she was drinking if he hadn't seen her drink, and he testified that he could smell it. I could see the wife frantically pulling at the lawyer's right sleeve and I heard her whisper to him, "He's lying. You can't smell vodka," and the lawyer whispered back to her, "By Gawd, my wife can!"

In another case which stands out in my memory, a farmer was suing his neighbor because his barking dogs kept him and his family awake at night. The defendant's attorney had another neighbor on the witness stand who testified that the dogs didn't bother him, and he lived closer to the plaintiff. The attorney was standing close to the witness when he elicited that favorable testimony. Then he backed away from the witness and asked, "Mr. Jones, I am now standing about 25 feet from you, speaking in a normal conversational tone. Can you hear me okay?" The witness learned forward, squinted his eyes, cupped his hand behind his ear, and said, "Do which?" Case closed.

A lady employed me to get her a divorce and enumerated many reasons why she wanted a divorce. After I filed the complaint in court, she brought her mother to my office to give her deposition to corroborate her testimony. The mother was so outraged at her son-in-law that she was barely coherent. She wanted to testify about every misdeed he had made through the years. The mother's demands were much more stringent than her daughter's. One of the mother's demands was that he pay $1,000.00 per month alimony. The daughter said, "Mother, he doesn't make but $750.00 per month." The mother replied, "If he quit drinking and running around with women, he could afford to pay you." The daughter responded, "If he quit doing those things, I don't want a divorce."

In DWI cases, the defendant usually testifies that he has had a couple of beers; the police officer testifies that the defendant was "blind, staggering drunk; the defendant's mother testifies that her son never touches the stuff. Ah....what would we do without mothers?

I was trying an automobile case one time and one of my witnesses testified that he saw my client give a left turn signal. On cross-examination, he admitted that he was over 100 feet away at the time. When the defense lawyer asked him just how far he could see, he said, "I don't know. I can see the moon. How far is that?"

Chapter 25:
His Honor

In 1975, one of chancery judges was appointed to the federal bench, and I aspired to get Governor Pryor to appoint me to finish out the term which expired on December 31, 1976. A Jonesboro attorney also wanted it. Craighead County had more lawyers than any other county in the Second Judicial Circuit. We each had friends working in our behalf. The president of the Northeast Arkansas Bar Association decided to call a meeting, on short notice, to be held in Jonesboro in Craighead County. The attorneys in attendance voted by secret ballot. I never learned how the final tally came out, but I got the appointment and got my shirt-sleeved picture on the front page of the <u>Arkansas Gazette</u>. I took leave from the law firm, intending to return on January 1, 1977.

In December of 1976 a circuit judge died, and I had done a good enough job as chancery judge that the lawyers asked me to serve out that term as circuit judge to expire December 31, 1978. I took another leave of absence from the firm and liked the circuit bench (with jury trials) so much that I got one of the other circuit judges to run for my division so I could run for his. I drew no opponent so I sailed through two four-year terms without a political campaign. I served until I was eligible to retire on December 31, 1986.

In 1975 a trial judge made about $30,000 per year, so I took quite a cut in pay. Top attorneys did not want the job. Since I did so little criminal work as a trial lawyer, after I became a judge, I spent most of my time trying criminal cases, which were much more interesting and challenging that civil cases. My court reporter and I alternated driving our cars. We covered ten courthouses: Piggott, Corning, Paragould, Jonesboro, Lake City, Harrisburg, Wynne, Osceola, Blytheville and West Memphis.

On pre-trial day in Mississippi County the defendants were brought to court in handcuffs and chained together. The courtroom would be full and they would be paraded before me all day, some pleading not guilty and others disposed of on negotiated pleas. I would process 30 to 40 cases in one day. One time I did not get finished and went back the next day for the remaining cases. When I got out of my car and started walking to the courthouse, I saw a nicely dressed elderly lady walking toward me. When we were about 15 to 20 feet apart, she said, "Good morning, Your Honor. Thank you for what you did yesterday." I had no idea what she was referring to but I was smiling and bowing, and just as I drew even with her, she looked me in the eye and said, "You son-of-a-bitch." I was so stunned that she disappeared around the corner before I came to my senses. My court reporter thought her daughter's rape case was disposed of on a negotiated plea the day before and she apparently did not like what happened.

One time in Harrisburg when the courtroom was full of people, a huge black man was being escorted down the aisle by the sheriff in front, and a deputy handcuffed to the prisoner following behind the sheriff. The defendant knocked the deputy down with his free fist and was bending over trying to get the handcuff loose. His back was to the sheriff. All the sheriff could get hold of was his prison pants which were held up with elastic. When the sheriff pulled down on the pants, everyone could see that he wore no underwear. It was quite a spectacle. Mooned in vivid color in broad daylight.

Before I went to the bench in 1975, judges in our circuit did not wear judicial robes and ran court rather informally. I changed all that. I told the bailiffs to open court with a "Hear ye, hear ye, all rise" etc. One dumb bailiff in Harrisburg tried to comply but it came out, "You'ens all git up now."

At court in Paragould, one of the jurors had a well known "bottle" problem. When we convened after lunch the bailiff told me that the juror appeared to be drunk. He was seated in the front row and I told him to stand up. I asked him whether he had been drinking. As he tried to explain that he had one beer with his hamburger, he fell forward over the jury rail onto the court reporter's table. He sobered up in jail.

While I was judge, the legislature passed a tough DWI law which was badly needed. I held one section to be unconstitutional, but the press played it up that I had struck down the whole new DWI law. An old lady yelled curses at me the next day when I was jogging, and I got a letter from a penitentiary inmate thanking me and observing that it was "about time somebody took up for us drunks."

During a hearing on a divorce case, the husband testified that his wife nagged him so much he could not eat or sleep and had lost 40 pounds. While he was sitting on the witness stand, there was a break in the action while the attorneys were doing something, and he turned to me and said, "You are so slim. Your woman must be a nagger too, with you havin' a settin' job and all."

One time when I was holding court in Piggott, I was walking from my car to the courthouse carrying my judicial robe on one arm and my briefcase in the other. There were some old men sitting out under a tree playing checkers and I overheard one of them say, "That there's Jess Brown's boy." Another one said, "It is? What's he do?" and the other man said, "Oh, I think he's some kind of lawyer or something."

The most unusual case that ever came before me as judge was tried in Wynne. A blind boy was pushing a quadriplegic along the street in a wheelchair and the quadriplegic spotted a car that had the ignition keys in it, and they decided to steal the car. The blind boy put the quadriplegic in the passenger seat, folded the wheelchair up and put it in the rear seat, and the blind boy sat in the driver's seat. The quadriplegic furnished the vision and the blind boy operated the brakes and steering wheel. They got as far as Helena before they had a wreck and got caught. The jury sentenced them to three years in prison, and I called the Department of Corrections to find out if they would be able to accommodate people with those handicaps, learned that they could, so I sentenced them accordingly.

Cross County, whose county seat is Wynne, was taken out of our judicial circuit and I missed going there because when they remodeled the judges' quarters in the courthouse at Wynne, the plumber had mistakenly arranged the pipes in such a manner that there was hot water in the judges' commode, which felt pretty good on a cold morning after a 75 mile drive.

Chapter 26:
Retirement

The decision to retire was a difficult one. I was a workaholic and did not know what it would be like to loaf. After I retired, I noticed that my jokes were not as funny. When I was on the bench, the attorneys laughed uproariously at all my jokes. At first I refused to get involved in volunteer work. I was on the hospital board and two or three committees but that was all I did, except play golf. About five years after I retired, our hospital built a new critical care unit and I volunteered to recruit enough volunteers to man the waiting room seven nights a week, and Saturdays and Sundays. I have regulars and a list of substitutes I can call when a regular can't work.

Starting in 1972 I became involved with a small group of people who were trying to save and restore the old courthouse, since we were building a new one. I have spent hundreds or, perhaps, thousands of hours working to restore the old Greene County Courthouse that was built in 1888. Some people wanted to tear it down and build the new one on the site. Mary Ann Schreit and I and others begged the quorum court to give us a year to see if we could restore the old courthouse without asking the county for any money. We did some investigation and found out that we could get some matching funds from both the federal and state governments. A year later, we went before the quorum court again and told them we could restore it without asking the county for any funds, and I remember there was a close vote. It was only when County Judge David Lange voted in our favor that we were able to save the old courthouse. We promised the county that the project would be completed in three years but it took 18 years and lasted until the year 2010, and occupied most of my time.

Much to my and Lottie's surprise, I raised ten times more money than all the other workers combined. We always thought that Lottie was the salesperson and that I could not sell beer to a troop train. I suppose the prestige of judge was the reason for my success as a fundraiser.

I learned early on that a good technique was to appeal to a widow to purchase a plaque in memory of her deceased husband. I would mention one good deed her husband had performed; then ask her about others. Usually she would proudly describe his other community endeavors and pretty soon he was the pillar of stone upon which Greene County was built. I would observe what a shame it would be if a man of his stature did not have a fitting memorial in his honor. Then I would show her a sample plaque as she reached for her checkbook. Case closed.

The above plan was not entirely fool-proof. One time it blew up in my face. When I finished my sales pitch, the "widow" said, "My so-called deceased husband is still very much alive, living in Walcott with a whore. I kicked that son-of-a-bitch out of this house ten years ago, and if you don't get your skinny ass out of here, I'll do the same to you." I made a hasty exit.

Despite such setbacks, we raised over $500,000.00 locally from Greene County citizens and businesses, and we received over $500,000.00 from state and federal funds. The Greene County Courthouse Preservation Society voted to name the restored courtroom in my honor, and a plaque has been erected at the front door of the courtroom which reads, "Judge Gerald P. Brown Courtroom." I am very proud of that.

The old courthouse cost $14,700.00 to build in 1888, and during the marathon restoration process, we spent more than $1,000,000.00. Although the county still owns the land and the structure, it was leased for 99 years to the Greene County Courthouse Preservation Society, a not-for-profit corporation, which, in turn, leased to the Chamber of Commerce for a 25-year term with the provision that, as rent, the Chamber will maintain it. The Chamber occupies the ground floor, and the courtroom is used occasionally for court purposes even though we have three courtrooms in the new courthouse. It is used mostly by the Chamber for social functions.

I believe most people now feel that restoring the old courthouse was a worthwhile effort. I regret to say that two of the wealthiest men in Greene County opposed the restoration vigorously and didn't contribute anything toward the restoration. They probably still think it was a dumb idea and a fool's journey.

I also started helping Lottie help raise funds for the cancer drive and for the past couple of years I've spent much time and effort helping two bedfast neighbor ladies. When Bunny spent her junior year abroad (at Exeter University in Devon, England), Lottie and I took a cruise up the Rhine and left the tour when it ended in London. We road a train to Devon, rented a car and toured England with Bunny. When Cliff lived in Bavaria, Germany, we visited him and he took us on a tour of Italy, Austria and Germany. When Cliff lived in Low Laithe (near Harrogate), England, we visited him and house-sat while he went on holiday. Bunny joined us and we rented a car and toured Scotland and the Isle of Skye, staying at B&Bs and eating at pubs.

In 1989, Lottie and I went to China about one month before the Tiananmen Square uprising. About 1993 or 1994 we went on a cruise of the Danube River, boarding the ship at Budapest. We took bus tours of the city and country by day and sailed to another city by night (Romania, Hungary, Republic of Slovakia, Italy and Germany).

In 1995 we celebrated our 50th wedding anniversary by attending the French Open Tennis Tournament in Paris. In 1996 we went to Wimbledon in London. We visit Cliff in California and Ron in Virginia occasionally. We visited Bunny every other weekend when she lived in Little Rock.

When I first retired, I would take high school students to court and let them watch a trial. I would meet with them before we went to court and tell them about the case and, then, after the trial, I would explain why certain things were said and answer their questions.

I still remember enough of the poems that I memorized in 1936 that I can fill a 40-minute class period.

In 1997 Bunny decided to move to Paragould because she wanted her daughters, Emily and Anna Caroline, to attend public schools in Paragould rather than in Little Rock. She and the girls lived with us until they could find a house. She is a stockbroker for Dean Witter and her office is in Jonesboro. Bunny's husband, Stephen Lee, found a job in Paragould in July of 1997.

Ronnie's daughter, Lisy, graduated from the University of Arkansas and went to intern in Senator Pryor's office. She then got a paying job in Senator Bumper's office. When Senator Bumpers announced his plans to retire on December 31, 1998, Lisy worked for Betty Bumpers and Rosalyn Carter in the "Every Child by Two" program.

In June of 1997 we rented a beach house in Gulf Shores, Alabama. The whole family was there and we were having a good time until Hurricane Danny chased us out.

Lottie and I are now approaching our 66th anniversary and we've been living at 1204 Robinwood for almost 12 years.

I had a light heart attack in 1999. I underwent an angiogram, and I have two stents in one artery and one in another. I quit all my volunteer work and retired from the hospital board after 47 years of service. I quit jogging and started walking after the heart attack. I walk two to two and a half miles, four days a week, and do about 45 to 50 minutes of strenuous stretching exercise, three times a week. Lottie has learned to make delicious meals with fat free or low fat food and I keep my weight around 155 and am 5' 11" tall. I love to play golf, not very well, but I enjoy it, and play three or four times a week. Ron, Cliff, Stephen and Leonard can all beat me at golf.

Lottie is a cross-stitch expert and our walls are adorned with her handiwork. Most of them are really works of art and will become collectors' items some day, I have no doubt.

Now that I'm approaching my maker, my religious practice has intensified. I recently took a Bible course that included 144 hours of classroom discussion and four to five times that amount of homework Bible study. All who signed up for the Bible course were asked to state the reason they were taking it. I gave as my reason that I wanted to find a way for my Jewish wife to get to Heaven, even though she did not believe that Jesus was for real. I did find in First Corinthians, Chapter 7, Verse 14, some support for that. In general, it states that an unbelieving spouse was no reason to break up a marriage and, in fact, if the head of the household was a believer, then all who reside therein are sanctified. Our pastor observed, "Leave it to a lawyer to find a loophole through which to sneak his wife into the back door of Heaven." I would feel better if those words had been spoken by Jesus rather than Paul. I will admit that many of the stories in both the Old and New Testaments are so contrary to our experiences in life that they are hard to accept at face value, but even if the whole concept of Jesus is false or exaggerated, it is clear to me that the principles He stood for are so fundamentally sound and sensible and are, indisputably, a wise guide for the good life: to live in harmony with God and my fellow man and myself; love, peace, and justice; concern for widows and orphans and the downtrodden; everything Jesus advocated was for the common good and not the privileged. For most of my life, I had just enough religion to make me feel guilty, uncomfortable and miserable. Now that Bunny and her family attend church regularly, Stephen chairs the Board of Trustees at First United Methodist Church, and I go every Sunday and enjoy it. I get such a glorious feeling on Sunday morning that I feel like shouting like by grandma Brown did.

The most wonderful treat to my ears is to hear the word, "Poppy," when it is uttered by my granddaughters, Emily and Anna Caroline. I find that I'm closest to heaven on this earth, and my favorite moment happens, when, on the first Sunday of every month, I kneel at the altar between Emily and Anna Caroline and receive the Holy Communion.

I really feel sorry for the unchurched - like my wife and son, Cliff. I pray daily that they will find their way to Heaven. I believe that the reason our religious differences did not tear us apart is that we never discuss it. I respect her right to feel like a Jew. She does not attend services. I don't recommend mixed marriages such as ours, but our commitment to each other has been validated by 65 years of togetherness. I agree with the sage who observed that "long marriages are born when lust morphs into tolerance." It hampered my church attendance for many years, but I am now comfortable. I am so glad I took the Bible courses. The Old Testament stories are more interesting than a novel. I teach a Sunday School Class and that is my continuing Bible education. I especially enjoy the first five books of the Bible (The Torah). My daily prayer includes the Apostles' Creed, John 3:16, the Lord's Prayer, and the 23rd Psalm. I then lift up the ones in my prayer who are special to me or who have special needs, and then I travel in my mind the old road from Greenway to Mt. Zion Church (which no longer exists). I plow a few rounds in the field where I first plowed. The mules are already hooked to the plow when I arrive in my dream, and I follow the gravel road on to the house where I was born (which no longer exists). That is a nightly journey while I am trying to go back to sleep after my frequent trips to the bathroom.

An event occurred while I was in the Marine Corps, stationed in Samoa, that is too unusual to ignore. The First Lady, Eleanor Roosevelt, was scheduled to visit the Marines in Samoa, I believe, in Pago Pago, and shortly before her scheduled visit, the CBs (Construction Battalion), stationed on the island stole some rubbing alcohol from the dispensary and mixed it with coconut juice, making a powerful alcoholic beverage. They sold some to some Marines and, as I recall, 12 or 13 of the Marines died from drinking the potent stuff the night or day before Mrs. Roosevelt's visit. Since it would have looked very bad for the brass if knowledge of that tragedy became known, there was a frantic effort to keep Mrs. Roosevelt in the dark. Since I was in Headquarters Company, and, I suppose, considered part of management rather than the union, I was put in charge of several (12 or 15) gooks (native Samoans), and we dug enough graves in some out-of-the-way place on the island, and buried those dead Marines that night. I have no idea what explanation was given by the "powers that be" to the families of those deceased Marines, but I am sure it was not the truth. I am acquainted with a fellow, a former Marine, who lives in California and who was on Samoa the same time I was, and I am going to inquire of him what he remembers about the event. He is the same one who found about why we were kicked out of the V-12 Program, which, I believe, I have already described. He might know how to go about checking the Marine Corps' records to get information about the Eleanor Roosevelt episode.

Since the foregoing was dictated, my brother Don passed away under most grievous circumstances. He was 72 years old and in good enough health that he walked six miles every day and had quit smoking and drinking years ago, but, on a routine physical examination, a chest x-ray revealed a spot on a lung which turned out to be malignant. He entered the Northeast Arkansas Regional Hospital in Jonesboro on December 6, 2002, and underwent lung surgery whereby the top lobe of his left lung was removed, but the leakage of air into the chest cavity continued and he was operated on again two or three more times. Finally, on February

11, 2003, he died. About 10 years ago when he made out his living will he asked me whether he could name me as the one to make decisions about his treatment if he became disabled. His two sons both lived in Utah and his long-time companion, Sandy Hall, apparently was not eligible because they were not married and he was not related to her. I gave him permission. Since he was twelve years younger than I, it did not occur to me that I might ever have to make that decision. When it came time to decide when to pull the plug and terminate efforts to keep him alive, I had a tough decision - a daunting task.

At Don's funeral, I met Roy Brady, who reminded me of an episode that occurred many years ago. When I was about 14 years old, I would either walk or ride a horse to Pollard, Arkansas, to find a girlfriend, and I got acquainted with Roy who lived fairly close to Pollard. Sometimes we played baseball together. Roy did not have a girlfriend. One night I was spending the night with him and he told me that God had called him to preach the Gospel, and I was so touched by that information that I gave him my girlfriend, Ruth Nettles, and all the money I had in my pocket, which was one dime. Ruth and Roy married and Roy became a Baptist preacher and preached for many years. At the time of Don's funeral, Roy told me he and Ruth had been married more than 60 years and he had retired from the ministry.

Our son, Ron, has now remarried and his present wife's name is Angela and she has a five-year-old daughter named Morgan. They live in Perciful, Virginia.

In the fall of 2007, I was invited to speak to the senior class at the University of Arkansas Law School in Fayetteville. The tension associated with that endeavor precipitated another heart problem for me: atrial fibrillation, which simply means "irregular heart beat." I would be disabled again that time for about a year. I take coumadin and will do so for the rest of my life. Every time I break the skin, I bleed profusely and every little bump leaves a purple spot on my skin.

In 2008 a local man wrote and directed a movie entitled, "The River Within." The leading parts of the movie were played by professional actors, but many local people appeared in the film. Lottie and I successfully auditioned for speaking roles, and were the only locals who had that honor. The movie is on DVD and hundreds of copies have been sold.

In 2009 as I approached my 90th birthday, I sensed that my mind was dimming. In an effort to delay the onset of senility, I started taking piano lessons and working crossword puzzles. I took piano lessons for about a year and learned the basics--the notes--and I can play a few simple tunes, like "Clementine," "The Marine Hymn," and "Yankee Doodle Dandy." I spend a couple of hours a day working crossword puzzles and I think my mind is benefitting from these practices.

All of my life I have had frequent colds and always tried to minimize conditions that I thought caused my colds: like getting too cold, too hot, too wet in cold weather, etc. I am now convinced that colds are caused by someone else's cold germs--not the elements. When our resistance is high, we are not susceptible and, thus, repel those cold germs. Everyone is exposed to someone's cold germs every day, but succumb only when our resistance is low. The best defense, therefore, is: eat healthy foods, exercise, sleep well, and get plenty of rest. It took me many years to learn that lesson.

The April 2010 edition of the Premiere magazine, locally published, has my picture on the front cover. Inside there is an article about my background and community work. I don't know how many copies are printed, or how wide the distribution, but I have received telephone calls from Jonesboro, Piggott, Rector, Corning and Kennett from friends who saw the magazine. That article was contemporaneously published with the dedication of the courtroom in the old courthouse, which event was covered by Channel 8 TV, KAIT News, in Jonesboro.

As a result of all the recent publicity, I am currently riding a wave of popularity. 'Tis a pity I'm not running for public office. I am writing this in May of 2010 at a time when the airwaves are filled with political supplications. I even received a call from James Roosevelt, grandson of President Roosevelt, soliciting my vote for a candidate for the U.S. Senate. Lottie also received a call from him, and I have heard that others did too.

In the publication of the Premiere magazine just mentioned, Lottie had a recipe for a cake and because of a misprint, the recipe called for "chicken broth" as one of the ingredients. One lady called up and wanted to know whether she puts chicken broth in her cake recipe because she is Jewish. Of course, Jewish mothers have a wide reputation for doctoring everyone's ills with chicken soup - a veritable panacea.

Recently, when I was shopping in Wal-Mart, a chubby lady, who appeared to be about 55-ish, touched me on my shoulder and asked me if I was Mr. Brown. She then told me her name and related an incident about which I have no memory. When she was six or seven years old, her daddy ran off with another woman. Apparently, there was litigation involving custody of the children, the lady talking to me and her little brother. I represented her mother and some "mean lawyers from Jonesboro" represented her father. We won the case and she was so glad that she and her brother did not have to go live with that other woman. She exclaimed about how kind I was to her mother; how often they had prayed for me during all these years; how sorry she was that her mother had died before she found me, etc. That encounter gave me a good feeling to know that I had been such a blessing to someone.

Chapter 27:
Grand Marshall

The good Lord continues to bless me. As I wrote what I thought would be the last paragraph of this book, a phone call changed my plans. I was notified that the movers and shakers of this town had chosen me to be the Grand Marshall of the 2010 Christmas Parade, sponsored by the Paragould Chamber of Commerce. That prestigious honor is bestowed upon the person who, the committee feels, has done the most for the betterment of this community of 22,500 people. My volunteer work on the hospital board for 47 years, on the restoration of the 1888 courthouse for 18 years, and my efforts to improve the quality of education in grades one through twelve, were cited as factors. I appreciate this recognition. In the words of Yogi Berra, "I thank all of the people who made this night 'necessary'."